PAPIER-MÂCHÉ ARTISTRY

Other Art Books by Dona Z. Meilach

IN THIS SERIES:

MACRAMÉ: CREATIVE DESIGN IN KNOTTING
CONTEMPORARY STONE SCULPTURE
CONTEMPORARY ART WITH WOOD
DIRECT METAL SCULPTURE
with Donald Seiden

ALSO:

CREATING ART FROM ANYTHING
CREATIVE CARVING
CREATIVE STITCHERY
with Lee Erlin Snow
CREATING WITH PLASTER
MAKING CONTEMPORARY RUGS AND WALL HANGINGS
PRINTMAKING
PAPERCRAFT
COLLAGE AND FOUND ART
with Elvie Ten Hoor

APPLE TREE PLAQUE. Dona Ziegler. Paper relief shapes on a papier-mâchéd backing of wood.

ELEPHANT. Conny von Hagen of Alcoa. Made over an aluminum-foil armature, shaped, then papier-mâchéd with printed tablecloth.

Courtesy, Aluminum Company of America

HEAD. Gemma. Papier-mâché from a mold is given a ceramiclike finish.

Collection, Mr. and Mrs. Saul Hurwich, Lincolnwood, Illinois

CHEST OF DRAWERS. Papier-mâché decorating over a painted wood chest.

Photographed at Sala de Artes, Mexico City

Dona Z. Meilach

PAPIER-MÂCHÉ ARTISTRY

London
George Allen & Unwin Ltd

For Gemma Taccogna,
for bringing papier-mâché
to a new artistic level

FIRST PUBLISHED IN 1971

PRINTED IN THE UNITED STATES OF AMERICA
SBN 0 04 745003 7

Acknowledgments

Tracking down the finest examples of contemporary papier-mâché has taken me to several cities in the United States and to Mexico, where I was warmly welcomed and met with enthusiastic cooperation.

In Mexico, artists and galleries permitted me to photograph their collections, and I especially want to thank Jeanne Valentine, San Miguel de Allende; Señora Sol Quadalajara of Los Castillo, and Señor Artus Filler of Sala de Artes, Mexico City.

In California, Lee and Herb Snow and Bob and Dorothy Courtney opened their homes so papier-mâché artists could bring their work for photography. I am also indebted to Gemma Taccogna who spent hours with me and my tape recorder revealing details on how she achieved the finishes which made her work unique. Lucy Anderson's home was a veritable museum of creative papier-mâché, and she gave me full rein to photograph the myriad displays.

Special appreciation to Chicago designer Bob Lee who helped develop many of the fine examples; to Conny von Hagen and the Aluminum Company of America for use of their unique furniture and ideas for foil. I am also indebted to Gus Leep of Illinois Bronze Paint Company, Lake Zurich, Illinois, for his technical advice about paints and to Judy Martin, also of Illinois Bronze, for sharing photos of outstanding work.

Several teachers assigned student projects and I particularly want to thank Carol Briscoe, Fry School, South Stickney, Illinois; Karlo Harootunian, Fairview South School, Skokie, Illinois; and Lorraine Ohlson, Proviso East High School, Maywood, Illinois. Thanks, too, to all the students and individual artists whose names, where known, accompany their work.

Ben Lavitt, of Astra Photo, Chicago, as always, has given my photo problems an extra touch of tender, loving care. Marilyn Regula has contributed her typing expertise in preparing the final manuscript.

Above all, my thanks to my husband who lugged camera equipment around Mexico and helped with photography, to my son Allen, for shooting photos while I developed many projects; and to my daughter, Susan, who spent an entire summer helping me experiment with the many papers, decorating techniques, paints, and finishes that proved most successful for papier-mâché.

Dona Z. Meilach

Palos Heights, Illinois

Contents

List of Color Plates

Foreword

As you thumb through this book, you may think that so many and varied examples require a great deal of know-how. Actually, the opposite is true. All examples are created by one of three approaches to papier-mâché; all involve only four simple procedures.

Rather than repeat the procedures with each project, the book is organized so that Chapter One describes the basic steps for all papier-mâché, with various ideas for decorating and painting. Chapters One, Two, and Three each delve into one of the three approaches. Therefore, for all examples, use Chapter One as your reference chapter; Two and Three for further development ideas. Chapters Four to Seven offer additional exciting applications for the approaches and procedures. Where the development of a piece is not so obvious, it has been demonstrated so you can readily follow the steps that lead to the finished piece.

Once the basic steps are learned and the procedures practiced, feel free to use the medium in any expressive and decorative manner you like. The same methods are equally valid in the classroom, the home, the artist's and decorators' studios.

All items are illustrated to familiarize you with the growing activity and possibilities of papier-mâché. You may wish to create some of the same pieces yourself. Or you may use the ideas as a springboard for further exploration of this revitalized ancient art medium. Be inventive in the objects you create and in combining and interchanging any of the approaches. Papier-mâché can be as exciting as its potential is unlimited.

PAPIER-MÂCHÉ ARTISTRY

PEOPLE CHAIRS. Conny of Alcoa. Aluminum foil shaped and mashed over a chair provides the armature for the papier-mâché medium of paper towels and paper tablecloths. Hands are shaped to hold dishes, glasses, and flowers. Dress them any way you like. More furniture ideas with papier-mâché in Chapter Six.
Courtesy, Aluminum Company of America, Pittsburgh

Introduction:

The Versatility of Papier-Mâché

Papier-mâché is one of the most versatile art media in popular use today. With it, one can create items as small as a bead, button, or earring, or as large as a monumental sculpture or architectural stage setting. It is invaluable in the home for making unusual decorative objects; in every art studio for developing relief shapes and three-dimensional sculptures; in the classroom at every grade level.

Papier-mâché has been used for centuries, yet contemporary artists and craftsmen have discovered innovative applications for the ancient material. In addition to newsprint, most often associated as the paper for papier-mâché, they use paper toweling, printed gift wrap, aluminum foil, and a range of art papers in combination with modern bonding agents and acrylic resins for finishing. The results, shown throughout this book, confirm the potential of the new approaches.

The Chinese were probably the first to use papier-mâché; later, the Persians and Japanese used it mainly for masks and festival objects. The widest application, however, was in Europe during the seventeenth century, and it is from the French that the term itself derives: "papier" meaning paper, and "mâché" meaning to masticate or reduce to a pulp. By the eighteenth century, England had a brisk papier-mâché industry, which in the nineteenth century supplied boxes, trays, tables, and furniture, often inlaid with mother-of-pearl, to the Victorian-styled homes. Many of these examples may be found in museums. One historian attributes the decline of English papier-mâché furniture to the heavy crinoline underskirts worn by women of the day. So much starched fabric tended to knock over the lightweight chairs.

Papier-mâché survived in early America, not as a trade as it had in England, but as a craft practiced by women who made boxes, plaques, lamps, and other utilitarian objects. Paper was cheap, and it was better to make use of it rather than discard it. It was perishable, however, so few examples exist today.

MASK FOR THE BLIND. Tibet. 19th century. Papier-mâché objects used for festivals often incorporated cultural symbolism. This mask represents a man whose eyes were put out as punishment for a crime. Later he was found not guilty. A new set of arms with eyes painted in the palms of the hands symbolize his "renewed eyesight."

Courtesy, Field Museum of Natural History, Chicago

By the twentieth century, more durable materials evolved along with industrialization. Manufactured items of wood, metal, plaster, plastic, etc., were preferred to handmade objects so papier-mâché diminished. More often it was used as a classroom activity for young children to begin exploring art fundamentals. Stage designers and display artists and carnival-float makers probably employed it more than anyone for making highly decorative displays that really didn't get much use or abuse and had only to last a short time.

It was in Mexico that the medium had its grandest survival. Papier-mâché was a traditional means for creating highly colorful festival decorations. Most popular was the piñata, usually in the form of an animal that at Christmastime was filled with candy, then broken by

MASK OF A YELLOW DANCER. China. 19th century. Oversized masks for festive occasions usually were part of a total costume combining papier-mâché with fabric and other materials. This was worn by two men, bending over, who performed a traditional dance.

Courtesy, Field Museum of Natural History, Chicago

the children so the candy would spill out. Traditional dolls and masks also remained popular.

In the last few years, however, an entire new papier-mâché interest has grown which is directly attributed to several factors. More people than ever are interested in making things. In our highly industrialized society, one feels a sense of wanting to make something oneself, something unique, individually expressive, different. Never before has there been such interest in arts and crafts.

In addition, early in the 1960s, novel papier-mâché objects were being created in Mexico by an artist named "Gemma." They elicited new excitement. People often weren't sure whether the pieces were paper or ceramics. Gemma, who had been a successful, talented de-

JUDAS FIGURE. Mexico. Larger than life-size figures are used for a religious procession. Later they are destroyed by firecrackers built into them. Brightly decorated papier-mâché over a cardboard form.

Photographed at the Fiesta Mexicana, Field Museum of Natural History, Chicago

signer in New York, moved to Mexico with her husband and gradually developed beautiful and useful items of papier-mâché applying contemporary styling. They had no relation to Mexican festival objects; they were beautiful as decorations and works of art. As tourists brought the pieces home the demand for Gemma pieces grew. She conducted classes in Mexico and many students (a number of tourists among them) were captivated by the versatility of the medium in her hands. They made items for themselves, then gradually for an increasing number of small gift shops in many parts of the world.

Other Mexican artists began to emulate Gemma and develop their own styles. Soon a thriving industry developed, and papier-mâché objects were exported throughout the world. Japanese manufacturers followed suit so that gift shops today display a delightful assortment of manufactured papier-mâché objects.

However, there is still tremendous interest in handmade objects and for this purpose the advantages of papier-mâché are numerous. The

BOWLS FROM INDIA. Papier-mâché has been an important part of the economy of Kashmir, India. Objects are hand painted in remarkable detail with traditional motifs. They are so beautifully shaped and finished with gold-leaf interiors that they look like metal until you pick them up and realize how lightweight they are.

Photographed at Design India, Skokie, Illinois

SIGNS IN A MODERN IDIOM are made of art tissue paper saturated with glue, shaped, and painted. The dry paper is extremely hard and durable.

materials, mainly paper and glue, are familiar to everyone, readily available, and inexpensive. The techniques are simple yet so flexible that they allow infinite combinations and results. The same principles of good design and color apply as much to this medium as any other.

Paints and finishes are the same as those for any other artistic or practical application. But the idea of applying modern paint finishes to papier-mâché has resulted in even greater variety and durability. Acrylics, epoxies, polyurethanes, antiquing materials, and other chemical achievements are equally at home over glue-hardened paper as they are over wood, plastic, plaster, cement, metal, etc. In addition,

HEAD. Gemma. Highly glazed heads with a porcelainlike finish added a new scope to the possibilities of papier-mâché in the early 1960s. Such treatment took papier-mâché out of the festival-carnival connotation and brought it to use as a medium for individual and industrial exploration.
Collection, Mr. & Mrs. Saul Hurwich, Lincolnwood, Illinois

HEADS. Bob Lee. Made over Styrofoam wig stands with the faces built out with cardboard. One is a caricature; the other is painted with a finish that will glow fluorescent under black light.

epoxies and polyurethanes that are used for waterproofing and general outdoor application may also be applied to papier-mâché so that forms are weather resistant. Automobile lacquers with high glazes may also be used for a chinalike appearance and an almost indestructible surface finish. If desired, one can make a casting from a bronze or stone sculpture and re-create it in papier-mâché. The papier-mâché figure is less expensive, lighter weight, yet it can be given the very same finished appearance as the original.

As more artists, teachers, and craftsmen continue to recognize the versatility of papier-mâché, they are introducing it into their work.

TABLE REFINISHED WITH PAPIER-MÂCHÉ. Irene Nelson. Papier-mâché is a marvelous medium for renewing old furniture or for individually finishing any kind of furnishings. Squares of construction paper are glued, then painted so the top simulates the look of antique leather. The edge is glued drapery trim.

FUN FIGURES AND DISPLAY ITEMS. Bob Lee. Cardboard cones, paper cups, and circles of cardboard are taped together to create the basic shapes for all these figures. Papier-mâché gives them texture and solidity. Whimsical decorating transforms the mundane materials into works of art.

For clarity, the following three chapters deal with three basic approaches to papier-mâché: (1) placing papier-mâché over an existing object; (2) creating an armature and then working papier-mâché over this; and (3) using a mold to make the papier-mâché object.

For further simplification, the procedures have been broken down into four steps: applying the paper, sealing, decorating, and finishing. These are shown in detail in Chapter One, then variations given throughout the book. **For all chapters, one should use Chapter One for a basic reference chapter.**

The purpose of the book is to present the techniques, to offer stimulating ideas, and to encourage you to use the techniques and apply the ideas to create your own forms with papier-mâché.

SKELETON HEAD. Fred and Barbara Meiers. In this marvelous piece richly decorated with Mexican symbolism, the artists combine papier-mâché with all aspects of design, color, shape, dimension, and individual expressiveness.

Photographed at The Egg & The Eye Gallery, Los Angeles

Part One MATERIALS, PROCEDURES, AND APPROACHES TO PAPIER-MÂCHÉ

chapter 1

Papier-Mâché over Existing Objects

With the profusion of objects and multitude of decorating possibilities illustrated, one may feel papier-mâché is a complex art form. But whether you cover a chest of drawers, make a small piece of jewelry, or create a sculpture, there are only four basic procedures for working with papier-mâché. They are:

1) *Applying papier-mâché* with a paste or glue medium and allowing it to dry thoroughly.

2) *Sealing the surface* so paint coats are not absorbed by the paper and so that fewer coats of paints are needed to cover newsprint and drying.

3) *Decorating the surface* and letting the decorations dry. Reseal decorations. (Steps 2 and 3 may be reversed . . . decorations applied first and then the entire object sealed.)

4) *Finishing the object* by painting, then protecting the painted surface with a glaze such as polyurethanes, varnishes, waxes, etc.

These steps are covered in this basic reference chapter.

In addition, it is important to understand that there are only three approaches to using papier-mâché regardless of the infinite variety of finished objects. They are:

A) Covering an existing object with papier-mâché.

B) Placing papier-mâché over an armature to create a new form. An armature is built up of wire, boxes, foil, paper cups, etc.

C) Re-creating a shape by using a mold. A mold might be a bowl, basket, vase, pot, dish or one made from an original clay model, poured into plaster and then filled with papier-mâché.

With this in mind, Chapters One, Two, and Three each deal with one of the approaches. For all approaches, refer to Chapter One for basic papier-mâché procedures.

The first approach to papier-mâché consists of gluing papers over existing objects. Bob Lee sliced the face from a Styrofoam wig stand and replaced it with a mirror. He covered the stand with glue-dipped paper toweling for a rough texture, then finished it with a coat of white matte paint. Also shown is a cigar box, first covered with papier-mâché squares and then hand decorated.

GENERAL CATEGORIES OF MATERIALS NEEDED FOR PAPIER-MÂCHÉ

Before you begin working in any of the approaches, gather your materials. You don't require all of the following; simply select the materials you feel you want to begin with, then add and experiment with others as you progress. Generally, you already have most of the materials in the house, perhaps requiring only sealer or paint finishes.

For papers use one or more of the following:
  Newsprint, paper toweling, crepe paper, art tissue paper, construction paper, bogus paper (a heavier gray construction paper), gift wrap, gummed tape, papier pulp, or instant papier-mâché.

For bonding:
  Flour and water, wheat (wallpaper) paste, white glue, polymer medium, plastic cement, and/or combinations of these.

Papers used for papier-mâché are newsprint, bogus paper, construction paper, paper toweling, packing paper, gift wrap, crepe paper, art tissue paper, textured Oriental papers, instant papier-mâché, gummed tape, kraft papers, masking tape, etc.

For decorating:

Shirt or other lightweight cardboard, curtain trim, rope, yarn, string, wood trim, stones, found objects.

For sealing:

Any primer such as gesso, a water-base synthetic wall paint (Kemtone is one brand), lacquer, varnish, glue or plaster.

For painting:

Any of a variety of paints described on pages 18 and 32.

Also scissors, ruler, fine sandpaper, paintbrushes, paintbrush cleaner, and the object or armature that will be the basis of your work.

ABOUT PAPER SIZE

There are as many ways to work with papier-mâché as there are people who do it. Some craftsmen work with two-inch squares of

For bonding papier-mâché to an object use wallpaper paste (also called wheat paste) shown being mixed gradually into water; white glue, spray adhesives, polymer mediums, mending cement, or flour and water. Some may be used interchangeably, others for specific spot gluing.

The first approach to papier-mâché consists of covering an existing object, using its form as the basis, and decorating in a fantastic variety of materials with a multitude of combinations. Almost anything can be renewed or changed whether it's made of metal, wood, plastic, glass, cardboard, etc.

paper, others prefer long strips or large squares. Some use one layer of paper, others maintain three are essential: some use as many as eight layers. Newsprint is the most popular paper because it is inexpensive, easy to work with, and always available. Some craftsmen use heavier papers such as construction paper, watercolor paper, and paper toweling. Much depends on the effect they wish to achieve. Generally, all agree that torn edges glue better and result in a more interesting finished appearance than machine-cut edges.

ABOUT GLUES AND PASTES

Several kinds of bonding materials work well. Interviews with craftsmen, plus testing, prove that all the following glue media are satisfactory but there are some differences. Some glues adhere harder than others, so the purpose and kind of paper used must be considered. The following are most successful for almost any papers.

Flour-and-water paste: Begin with 1 cup of water, mix in about ¼ cup flour until the mixture is thin and runny. Then stir this mixture into 5 cups lightly boiling water. Gently boil and stir for 2 to 3 minutes. Cool until you can dip the paper into it.

Wheat paste: (For crafts it is packaged as wheat paste; but it is the same powder you buy in your hardware store as wallpaper paste.) Mix according to package direction, always adding the paste very gradually to water and stirring. For better results, add a few squirts of white glue to the wheat-paste mixture. Keep the mixture about the consistency of sour cream.

White emulsion glue (such as Elmer's, Sobo, Wil-hold): Dilute approximately ¾ part glue with ¼ part water. Store leftover glue in glue bottle for spot gluing where necessary.

Polymers and modeling paste: Use straight from bottle or can. Modeling paste may be thinned with water, then paper soaked for a paper pulp that dries to a rock-hard surface.

To glue, do what comes easiest for the type of glue, size of paper, and object to be covered. You can dip the paper in glue, then wipe off excess glue between fingers. You can brush the entire surface with glue, then adhere the papers, always brushing more glue on papers where edges overlap. Always brush a coat of glue over a finished layer of paper to eliminate any lumps and catch any unglued edges. Heavier papers may be worked more easily if they are soaked in water a few minutes before placing in the glue medium and adhering.

Feel free to use any of the materials suggested; only a little experimentation and experience will be needed in order to decide what you like best. Some mixtures, stored in airtight glass jars or plastic containers, will be usable for a few days.

ABOUT DRYING

Glued papers and decorations must be dried thoroughly before sealing and again before painting. The amount and kind of glue, the numbers of layers of paper, and the weather determine drying time. Single layers of newsprint dipped in any glue will dry in a few hours unless the air is very damp. Heavier papers, several layers, and built-up forms may require anywhere from overnight to days of air drying. Drying can be hastened by putting objects in the sun, on a warm radiator, or in front of a warm forced-air vent. Always prop or hang a piece so air circulates freely around it. You can also place the object on the lowest shelf in the broiler of a gas oven. Do not turn on the oven; the heat from the pilot light is sufficient to hasten even drying.

Force drying may also be done by placing the object in the baking compartment of an oven at low temperatures. However, watch the piece carefully so it doesn't burn.

When wallpaper paste is used, dry as quickly as possible. It has been known to mold and become wormy and rancid if left damp too long in a musty basement.

ABOUT SEALERS AND PAINTS

A few words of caution about sealers and paint finishes are necessary. With the great variety of paints and the number of manufacturers, there is a factor called "paint incompatibility." This means that some finishes will not work satisfactorily when covered with other finishes. For instance, on one project enamel was used to cover papier-mâché, but when spray lacquer was applied, it caused the enamel to wrinkle or sag. Therefore, it is always wise to keep an extra few square inches of your project worked on a "sample" piece of cardboard or scrap of wood for preliminary testing. (Or try out products on a corner of the work.) After sealing your paper, test subsequent paint finishes to pretest their compatibility. Apply the same sealer and base coat. Use only small portions of your sample at a time should it be necessary to test several products. It's discouraging to cover an entire piece of furniture with papier-mâché squares, seal and decorate and paint it, and then apply a final glaze that may completely lift off the underpaint.

Always read and follow all directions on product labels and generally allow more drying time than the manufacturer suggests.

Approach No. I

Covering an existing object; the object remains permanently under the papier-mâché.

STEP NO. 1: Applying Paper

a. Often the size, shape, and direction the paper is placed contributes to the design of the item. Paper should be *torn* evenly into desired-size squares; remember to tear off machine-cut edges, too. Torn edges are generally preferred, though some people like the appearance of controlled cut edges. To tear, mark the paper off into widths desired, then tear evenly using a straight edge. Here, 2-inch strips which will be torn into 2-inch squares are being torn from bogus paper, an art paper often used for chalk drawing.

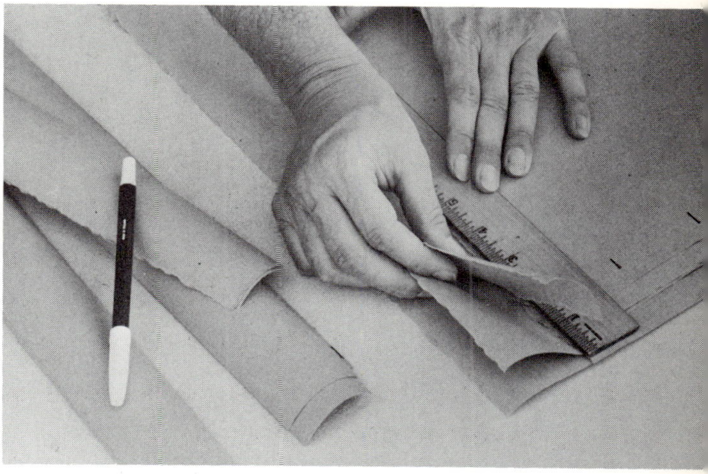

b. In addition to squares, an object may be covered with sheets of paper toweling shown being glued over a wood tray.

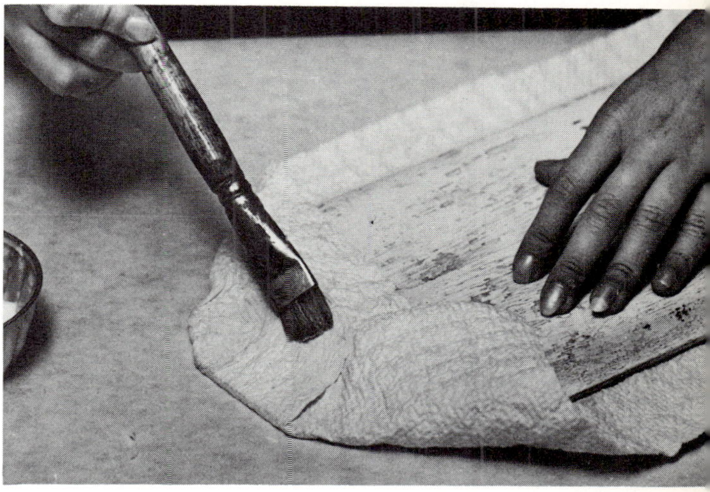

c. Or with circles of textured packing paper for another effect.
Always dry glued papers thoroughly before sealing.

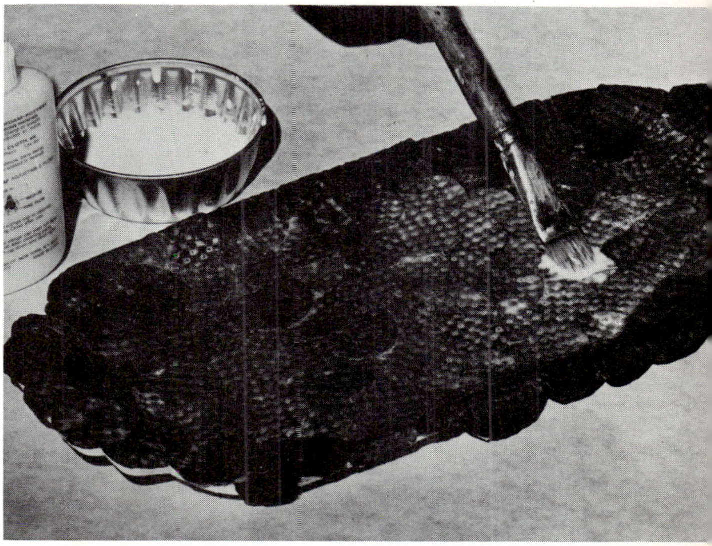

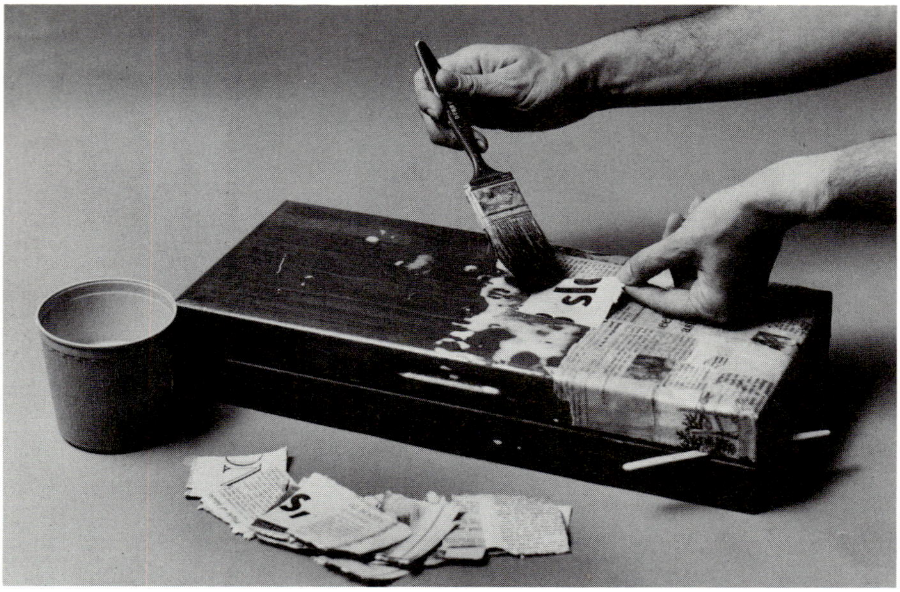

Newsprint is the most popular paper for papier-mâché because of its abundance. To cover this old, scratched wood silverware chest, 2-inch squares of torn newspaper are overlapped in even rows. The lid is propped open so glued papers on top and bottom do not adhere to each other. Wrap paper around lid edges and ends rather than lining up a paper edge at edge of box. Miter corners.

Dip paper completely in glue and wipe off excess, or brush glue on box and then on overlapping edges of paper which has been water moistened and lightly dipped in glue. Dry completely.

No matter what the object, paper is applied first to obliterate an old surface. An old metal tray is renewed with 1″ x 2″ squares of construction paper glued in a radiating pattern. Thicker papers accentuate overlapped, roughly torn edges for greater surface interest.

Torn paper may also be applied in thin strips. It is immersed in glue, then excess squeezed out between two fingers.

STEP NO. 2: Sealing

It is always good practice to seal paper surfaces. Sealing (also called priming) prevents paint from being absorbed by porous papers and prevents the print of the paper from bleeding through the paint. It minimizes the number of paint coats required and imparts an extremely hard finish to the paper that may be sanded if necessary. The three best sealers are gesso, straight white glue, and acrylic latex wall paint.

Gesso originally was made from gypsum or plaster and commercially prepared for use in painting by adding water, whiting, oils, and varnish. Michelangelo used a form of gesso to paint the Sistine Chapel, but modern gessoes have an acrylic latex base which dries fast, provides a tough surface and smooth application. Gesso is a white, opaque product that is brushed on and dries stone hard. One coat is usually sufficient for covering and sealing newsprint so the oils of the print will not bleed through subsequent paint coats. It will not obliterate torn paper edges. It may be used as it comes from the can or thinned with water. To avoid its drying out, always keep the can closed when not in use.

For very smooth finishes that hide paper edges, use six to eight coats of gesso, drying between coats and sanding the final coat. Brush on two coats of undiluted white glue to produce a porcelain- or ceramic-like finish so popular for contemporary papier-mâché. If a ceramic appearance is desired, one may ask, "Why not simply create the piece from ceramics?" The answer is that papier-mâché is less expensive than ceramics, requires no clay, no kiln-firing procedures, is lighter weight and less fragile. For a colored ceramic finish mix temperas with the white glue using about four ounces of temperas to one ounce of glue.

Gesso may be mixed with water-base colors such as temperas and

After the one layer of papier-mâché squares has dried overnight, the cutlery box is sealed to cover the newsprint, to create a nonporous surface for subsequent coats of paint, and to prevent oils from the inks from mixing with and bleeding through the paints.

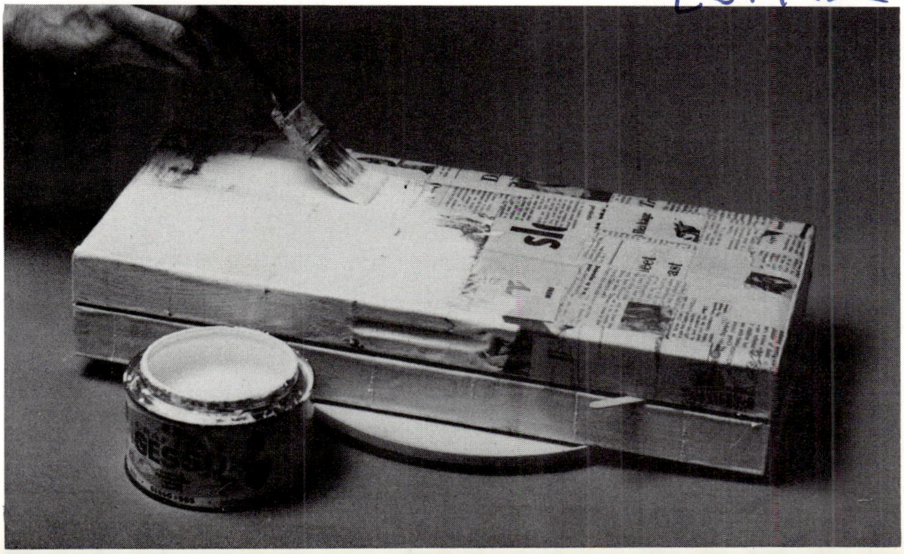

Mirror in progress. Lucy Anderson. A piece of corrugated cardboard set into a picture frame has a dish, placed upside down, glued to it. A round mirror is glued to the "foot" of the dish. All surfaces (except mirror) are papier-mâchéd and decorated with string and paper leaf shapes. It is sealed with two coats of gesso before proceeding with finishing.

acrylics for undertones. Textures may be added by mixing sand with the gesso. A final coat of wet gesso also may be textured by striating the surface with a comb or a toothed tool used for clay and plaster.

Latex paints used for walls also make good sealers. Colored latex paints may seal and color simultaneously and are less expensive than craft paints. However, a quart is often the smallest quantity available.

Undiluted white glue will also seal but because it dries transparent, it will not obliterate newsprint. Unprinted newsprint sketch paper may be used, then sealed with white glue. Or, if the newsprint itself becomes the final design, it should be sealed only with white glue. Clear shellac or vanish may also be used if print is not to be obliterated.

Most materials to be painted should be sealed including decorative trims such as string, cloth, and cardboard. String dipped into undiluted white glue to adhere does not necessarily require a gesso sealer. Always allow sealer coats to dry thoroughly before painting.

Often it is easier to seal an object before decorating, so you have a solid background on which to work. However, one can decorate an entire object and then seal depending upon the decorations and your expertise. Relief decorations are often easier to work with when sealed first, then glued to the base surface.

Brushes used for water-base sealers such as gesso and latex should be dipped in warm water immediately and soaked for ten minutes or so, washed with soap, and dried. A single can of gesso or latex paint is inexpensive and ample for covering many objects. Setting the object on a turntable simplifies working.

Sealers may tend to crack or flake if used with slick papers. Roughen up the paper surface slightly with sandpaper or use cracks for "accidental" textures. Sometimes, drying thick coats of sealer too fast in a very warm room also will cause cracking.

STEP NO. 3: Decorating

Decorating papier-mâché objects is where you can let your individual expressiveness and color preferences go wild. You can tie together motifs from fabrics, repeat scrollwork from furniture, carry over a wallpaper design, outline a favorite object or pattern. A variety of decorating techniques and materials is developed on the following pages. Almost every trim used on examples throughout the book is a variation of the following methods whether the trim is flat or high relief.

There is no mystery to creating the variety of trims. Most of them are made of string dipped in glue or shapes of newspaper glued together to form flowers, petals, fruits, leaves, abstract designs. You will also find lace, drapery tassels, doilies, decoupage papers, seashells, stones, ready-made moldings, pasta, instant mâché, and plaster. By studying how the designs are made on the following pages, then analyzing those on the scores of examples, you'll realize how utterly simple it is to re-create designs shown or to develop your own. Use ideas from wallpaper and fabric patterns, children's book illustrations, magazine photos, artwork. Select details from photos for designing your own objects. Dare to be innovative and inventive: anything goes so long as you are the designer.

A few trims applicable to papier-mâché decorating are lace, string, foil shapes, wood molding, colored stones.

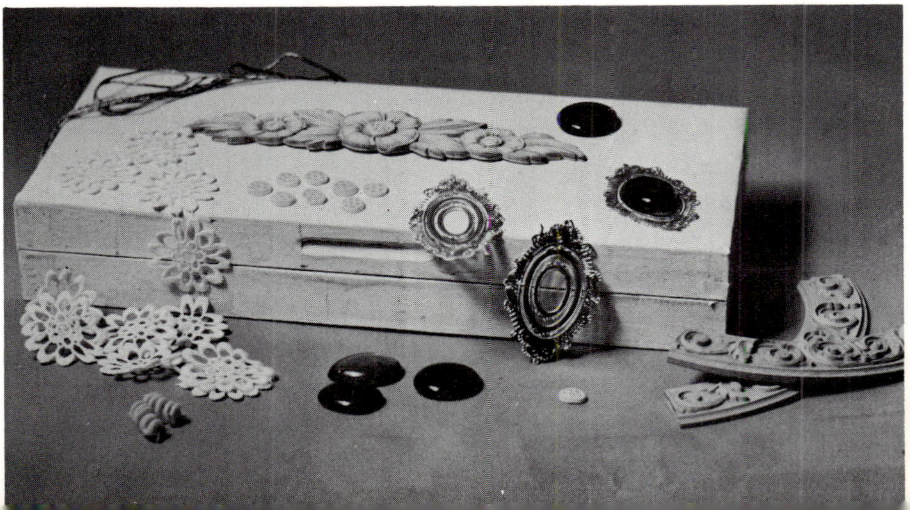

Decorating with string and cardboard

A simple way to begin decorating is to lay out your design on the box, sketch it lightly for placement, then dip your trims in glue and apply. Here, string and drapery trim are used. The center is composed of three different sizes and shapes of construction paper or cardboard placed on one another for a built-up form.

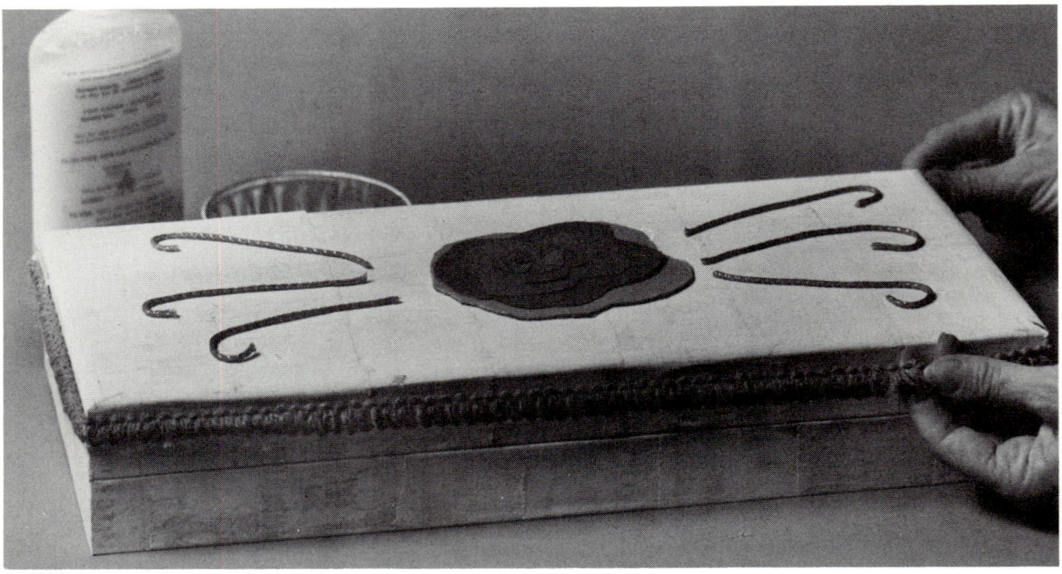

Strings and trims should be dipped in undiluted white glue, excess glue wiped off between fingers, then the trim applied. Hold in place a few seconds until string adheres as desired.

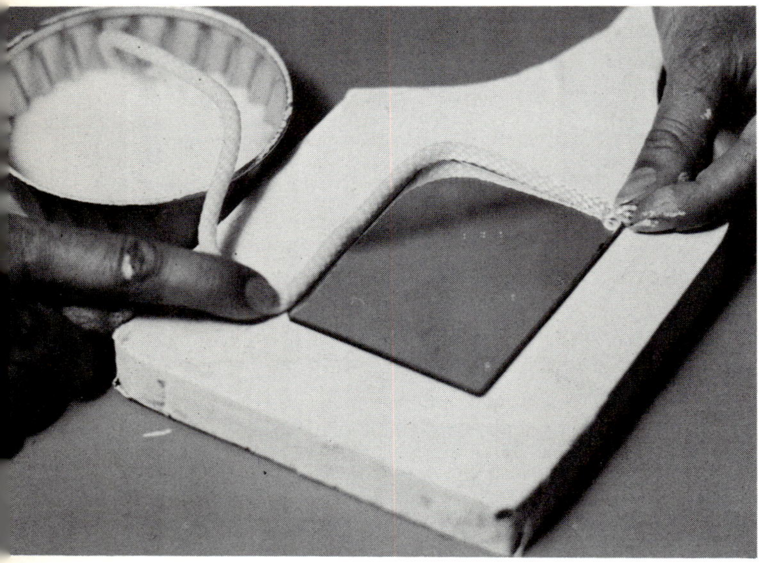

A thick cord is being applied to frame a mirror on a breadboard that will become a hand mirror.

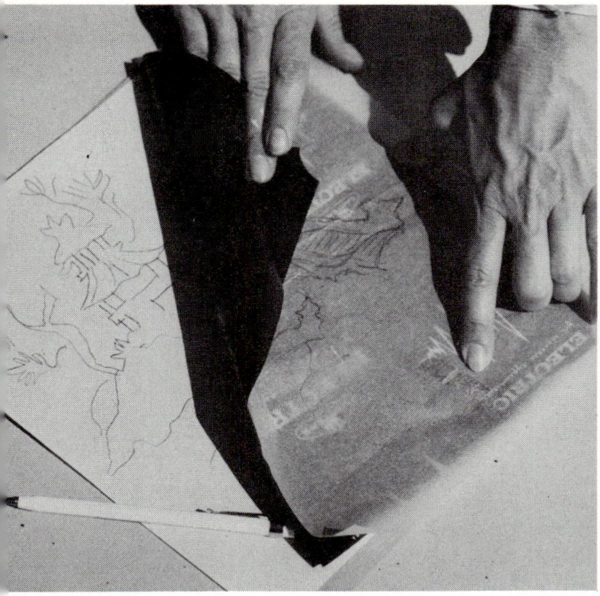

Design for a small chest (page 149) is made of cardboard relief and white seine twine. The design is sketched, then traced on a piece of shirt cardboard or white posterboard.

The overall shape is glued to the chest, then other shapes added where a build-up is desired. String is unraveled at ends to simulate branches.

Cardboard shapes are glued in place over ends of string for a higher relief that simulates a staircase.

After all glued areas are dry, the entire chest is sealed with a coat of gesso. Bogus paper was used as the paper medium.

Decorating with a relief buildup

To make a relief buildup of standaway shapes, the shapes are made separately, sealed, and then glued to the box. You can make almost any kind of shape for a relief by cutting out the parts from six layers of newsprint, gluing the layers together, then, while wet, shaping them to resemble leaves, cones, flowers, petals, etc. This is the same technique, used for jewelry, too, beginning on page 194.

Cut a design from six layers of newsprint and glue layers together. Make one slit from edge to center and overlap edges to form a slight cone. Tape at back. While form is wet from glue, mold with fingers and let dry. For a center, use a circle, another smaller layer of the same shape or a coil of fringed paper for a stamen. Dip paper in glue and roll or furl until stamen holds upright.

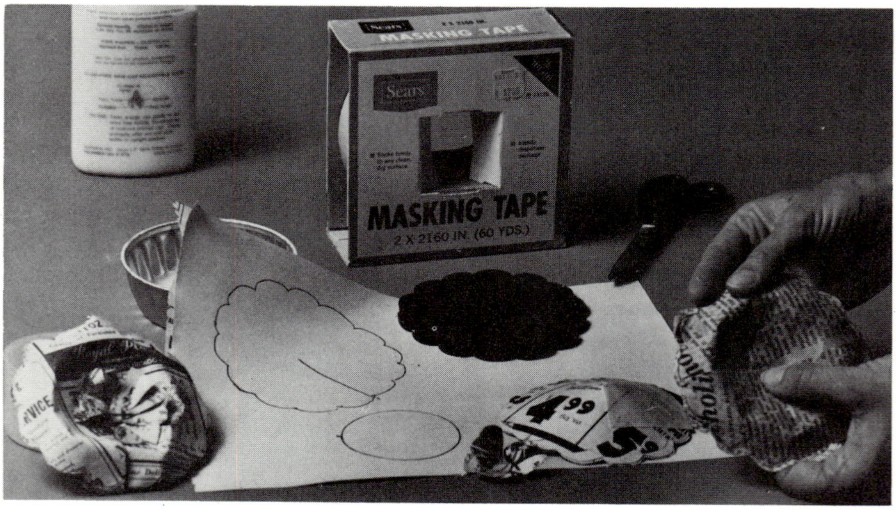

Individual petals may be formed over a layer of lightweight cardboard with newspaper glued to it. While glue is wet, shape petals, then overlap as desired to create flowers. Stem is made by twisting a narrow piece of art tissue paper and gluing in place.

Flowers and leaves made from newspaper layers add a three-dimensional quality to the top of a round cereal box decorated to camouflage cleanser in a bathroom.

Collection, Elvie Ten Hoor

A whole garden of flowers may be created from individual petals overlapped and painted, antiqued and highly glazed.

CASTLE. Myrna Greenberg. 24 inches high. To carry the idea of relief decorating a step further, one can do an entire work with overlapped pieces of cardboard, lace, paper, and cloth doilies. Wood dowels are used for window supports.

Details of castle. Myrna Greenberg. This same technique of overlapped cardboard shapes is used to make plaques: the demonstration is shown in Chapter Five.

To build up very high shapes on a papier-mâché form, one may also use modeling paste, plaster of Paris or Spackle. Modeling paste is a premixed, thick, artist's product ready for application. Plaster of Paris and Spackle, available at hardware and paint stores, are powders that must be mixed with water. All perform the same function. It is best to use them with some kind of border to hold the shape until it dries.

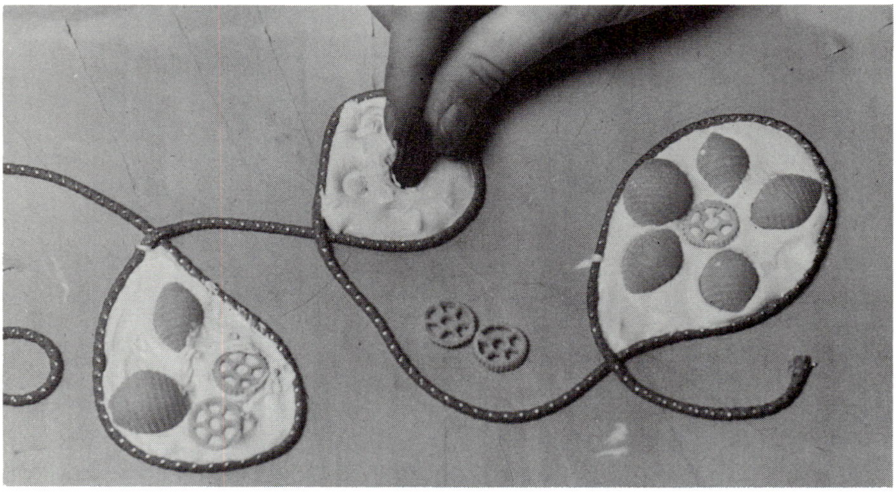

String, glued to the box in "doodle" fashion, creates a design and a border wall to hold the mixture which is spooned in and shaped with a knife. Pasta and seashells are embedded. Or, when the material "sets" slightly, impress designs with nails, bottle caps, hardware items, etc.

Instant papier-mâché is a commercially dried paper pulp product that, when mixed with water, has a claylike consistency. It dries hard in a few days. Mix according to directions. Stir until dry ingredients are moistened and hold together. Then knead (kneading is more efficient and less messy when done in a plastic bag). If too much water has been used, wrap lump of mâché in a paper towel to remove excess moisture.

Work instant mâché as clay to desired shapes for trims, details, etc. Lines may be etched into the surface before drying. Instant mâché dries rock hard in a day or so depending on thickness. If the dry shape does not adhere to the papier-mâché surface, attach with extra undiluted white glue. Objects may be set into instant mâché which will dry hard around them. Mâché also may be pressed around and between wires used for armatures.

Making your own paper pulp

Some people like to make their own paper pulp and the following procedure is basic: tear newspaper into small pieces about 1″ square and place them in a pan; cover with hot water and soak for several hours or overnight. When the pieces have been thoroughly soaked, squeeze and rub them as much as possible until they have been thoroughly broken down into a pulp. Place in a strainer and continue to mash until most of the water is removed. Then add wheat paste or white glue until a claylike consistency is reached. Use as clay either to build up a surface or to develop a solid three-dimensional shape. It may also be used to fill molds (see Chapter Three). Mix only as needed or the remainder will harden. Or store unused pulp in a plastic bag in a refrigerator for longer life.

For coarse pulp, use newsprint. For finer pulp use fine papers such as toilet tissue, facial tissue, or paper toweling.

STEP NO. 4: Finishing

There is a wide variety of paint products available for painting a background color, hand painting details, adding unusual tones and, finally, protecting.

After the sealer coat dries, you generally apply a background color with any paints sold for arts and crafts and for general painting. Water-base paints include poster paints, temperas, designers' gouache, acrylics, and a family of latex paints. Water-base paints generally dry quickly and brushes clean up with water. There are also oil-base paints such as artists' oils and general household enamels. Chemistry has, however, developed enamels with several valuable additives such as alkyd, epoxy, and polyurethane available for spray and brush on applications. All enamels have a tacky drying period of fifteen minutes to six hours and must be allowed to dry thoroughly before proceeding. They may be a matte or gloss finish and are available in a wide range of colors.

Lacquers have an acrylic or vinyl base and dry very quickly. They are touchy to use because they can lift an undercoat of enamel, causing it to wrinkle and sag.

For unusual touches there are antique Flemish sprays, crackle finishes, gold leaf, gold and silver paints, latex textures, metallics, fluorescent paints that will glow under black light, bronzing powders, etc. For fine line drawing, use India inks, ball-point and felt-tip pens, and colored pencils.

A wide choice of final protective coats are also available. Varnishes are made with polyurethane, epoxy, and alkyds which vary in price and usage depending upon the wear to which they will be exposed. For

Some paints, glazes, and novelty finishes available that are marvelous for papier-mâché.

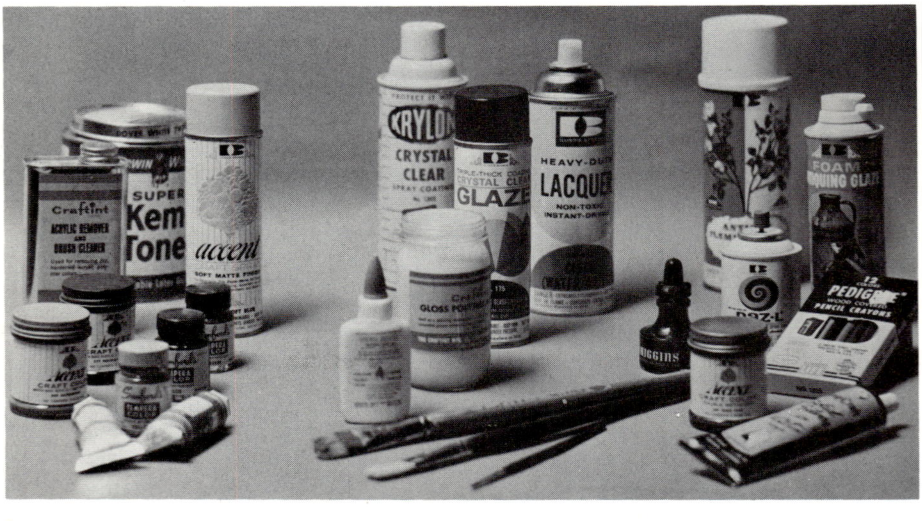

outdoor use, paints containing acrylic resins, polyurethanes, and epoxies will yield weather protection just as they would on the outside of a building or the hull of a boat. Some epoxy products are premixed for spray or brushing; some of the pigmented epoxies require mixing a catalyst with a color.

Paint brushes are important tools for papier-mâché. Buy broad brushes for sealing and painting, finer brushes for hand painting. Camel's hair brushes are often used for watercolors; stiffer synthetic bristles are sold for acrylics. Paint details with pipe cleaners or cotton swabs and simply throw them away after use.

Always clean brushes immediately so paints will not harden in them. Should brushes become stiff, there are special solvents for different media: acrylic solvents for water-base paints; turpentine or paint thinner for oil-base paints. Usually paint-can directions will recommend the thinner to use and this would apply to cleaning brushes also. After cleaning, reshape bristles and allow to dry by hanging up or placing handle of brush in a cup. Never rest drying bristles on themselves or they will bend and curl.

To familiarize yourself with the many paint products on the market, observe and read labels wherever paints are sold, such as craft and art shops and hardware and paint stores. A sizable mail-order catalog, such as Sears's or Ward's, is a good reference for the various paint finishes.

Experiment with products until you discover the differences and which paints are best for your purpose. Remember to keep a sample board going to pretest paints before using them on an entire project.

After the box has had all its final decor applied, it is regessoed and ready for finishing. The stem of the leaf has been made with a decorative silver semiliquid material from a tube.

An item may be spray painted. Spray paints are available in both matte and gloss finishes. Always spray paint in a well-ventilated room. Keep object in a box to confine spray and, if possible, on a turntable, so it is easy to turn for all-around spraying. To prevent paint from sagging and dripping, two light spray coats are usually better than one heavy coat.

Among the new craft products is a line of brush-on acrylic paints that perfectly match spray paints so you can touch up hard-to-spray areas. Or spray some paint into a waxed paper cup, then use the paint to brush on and touch up missed areas and details.

Details are hand painted with a brush, cotton tip, or a pipe cleaner. Freehand drawing may be done on areas of the box. Always dry each coat of paint thoroughly before painting additional coats or glazing. If a matte-finish paint has been used, and a high gloss is desired, the entire box is finished with a plastic glaze, varnish, or lacquer. When dry, it may be waxed with any good-quality furniture wax.

Depending upon the product and paint compatibility, novelty finishes may be applied either before or after glazing. An oil-base finish may not adhere well to a water-base finish, but usually the glaze coat will provide an adequate surface for a new medium. The object may be antiqued, sprayed with Pearl-glo or some other finish, then reglazed for a high gloss.

A plastic-base spray glaze adds a high gloss and a protective coat to the box.

CANNISTER SET AND TRAY. Lucy Anderson. The newspaper itself becomes the design used over plastic cannister set that has been glazed with white glue. White cord is used for flowers, glued around the rim, the cover, and the tops of the handles. Tray also has been covered with papier-mâché, then hand painted, rubbed with gold paint, and antiqued.

The types of items that can serve as a basis for papier-mâché are unlimited. Anything old or new is "eyed" by the papier-mâché artist as a potential for cover-up. That's what the whole art boils down to: being able to visualize what can be accomplished by the technique. On the following pages, you will discover several examples where objects have been used and simply covered up and renewed with imagination and papier-mâché. Also think in terms of combinations of objects such as the mirror that has the gesso coat on page 22 made from an upside-down dish and an old picture frame with cardboard set in. The combination of a dish and tray resulted in a new mirror shape that belied its origin.

In addition to found objects that can be covered, it is also possible to create your own boxes in any desired size and shape by cutting corrugated cardboard and making it into a box. Lids to fit may be shaped from cardboard. Handles of paper pulp or ready-made handles from a hardware store may be added. Paper-base boxes do tend to warp from the moisture in the glues and paints; they must be weighted with stones or tied with string to hold them in shape. With so many shapes available in our "throwaway society," a little scouting will usually turn up items you can cover so it's not necessary to make boxes. Cardboard can be used to fill in old picture frames and other shapes so long as it is supported to prevent warpage.

COFFEEPOT AND TRAY. Lucy Anderson. When the paper squares are applied in a carefully controlled radiating design, the newsprint itself provides an overall pattern. The matching coffeepot is simply decorated with hand-painted flowers. To make the set of matching snack servers, see Chapter Two.

DRESSER BOX WITH DRAWERS. Old chests may be found in secondhand shops or where unfinished furniture is sold. An artistic treatment can create a decorating focal point.

Facial tissue boxes can be individually decorated to match any color scheme. They can repeat colors and designs in wallpapers and fabrics for a completely coordinated accent in bedroom, bath or guest room.

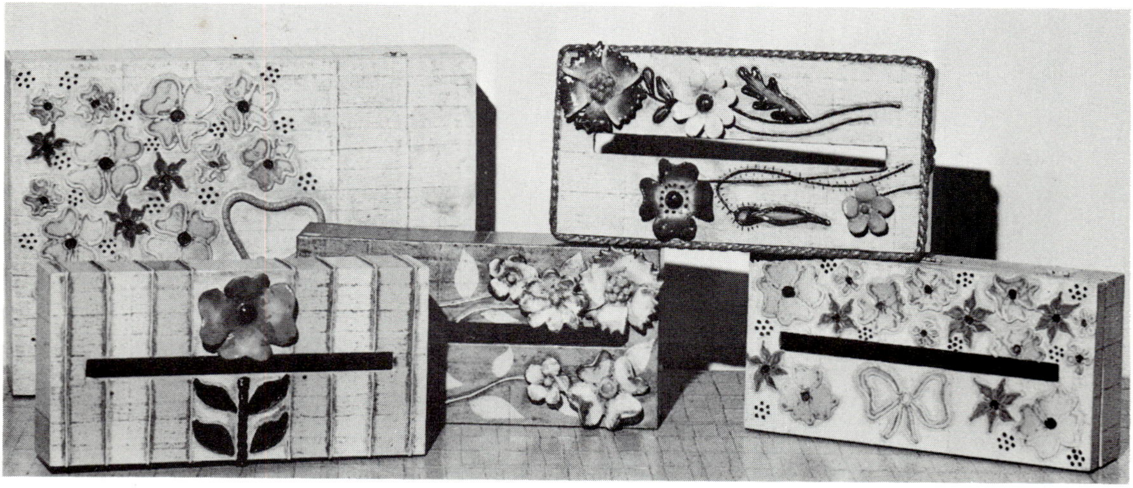

You can make this magazine rack yourself from wood or buy an unfinished one, then decorate it with papier-mâché.

Or a basket to use for wastepaper, umbrellas, magazines or ????

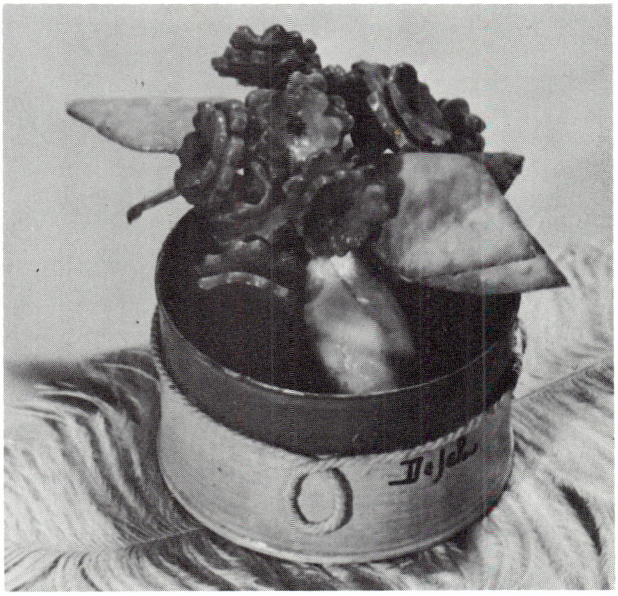

Or half a tin can with leaves and flowers of very thin Styrofoam glued together, wired, and attached to a wire stem.

Collection, Mr. & Mrs. Saul Hurwich, Lincolnwood, Illinois

Papier-mâché covered and decorated lipstick holders may be given many personalities.

They can be matched to a compact decorated with string and a cardboard face in the relief technique already shown.

To create a "head" on a tube of lipstick apply several thin strips of papier-mâché over the tube and extending over the top of the tube. Gather the strips together at the top and, while they are wet, roll them down, shape into a head and neck. Dry. Seal, sand, then decorate with string, hand paint, and glaze.

SUNBONNET LADY. Dona Ziegler. A real cotton bonnet brushed with glue to stiffen was stuffed and used for this lovely head complete with lace collar.

HEAD. Irene Nelson. A Styrofoam wig stand specially made with a long neck is covered with papier-mâché, then three coats of gesso for a smooth finish. The china appearance on the face is created by brushing on two coats of undiluted white glue. Then the piece is decorated and glazed. Decor consists of string and lace daisies.

Cover a metal lunch box that once held thermos and sandwiches for the children and make it into a beautiful jewelry box rich with surface decoration. Line the inside with felt or velvet. Handles and hardware have been removed.

Photographed at Sala de Artes, Mexico City

Another former lunch box has been magnificently covered with rows and rows of textured laces and trims. Paints and antiquing coats give it the appearance of a magnificent, heavily encrusted antique.

Photographed at Sala de Artes, Mexico City

LUNCH BOX PURSE. Irene Nelson. A battered lunch box had its life lengthened by papier-mâchéing and making it into a purse. The same hardware is used. The purse was lined with felt glued in the base and lid.

FLOWERPOT. Lucy Anderson. Made over a pressboard bucket that florists use.

Papier-mâché over a dish is combined with the decoupage technique. After the dish has been covered with papier-mâché squares and decorated with string, the center is the setting for a print that has been embedded beneath several coats of varnish. The result simulates a lovely antique in golds and blues.

Old bottles and vases are handsome flower holders when redone. Vase at left had its neck elongated by adding a cone of lightweight cardboard to the original bottle and camouflaging the joint with decorative cord.

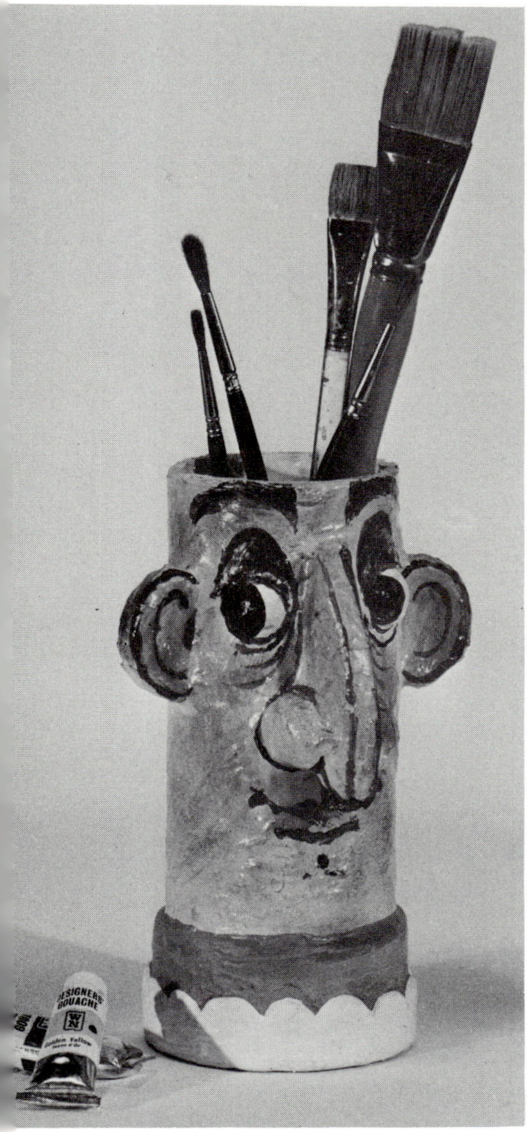

When designer Bob Lee needed a tall paintbrush holder, he took an old mug, covered it, handle and all, using the handle for a "nose" for his new friend. Ears were shaped from paper.

From Kashmir, India. Beautiful handmade papier-mâché objects are traditional. A humidor made over a metal can is intricately decorated.

Photographed at Design India, Skokie, Illinois

Candlestick holders and a hanging egg are also from India. One could create the same idea from lathe-turned wood spindles available at do-it-yourself centers and lumberyards.

Photographed at Design India, Skokie, Illinois

MIRROR. Lucy Anderson. With her inimitable ability to combine objects and create new shapes, Mrs. Anderson placed a dime-store mirror on a backing of cardboard cut to desired shape, then papier-mâchéd and decorated it to create an individualized, attractive object. One could also use another frame, or a piece of wood for the backing.

Mirror frame was covered with art tissue dipped in glue, then curled to shape. Bottom curls become the feet for the mirror which has a piece of cardboard glued to the back for a stand.

Photographed at Kroch's & Brentano's Bookstore, Skokie, Illinois

A pressboard floral bucket individually and beautifully decorated by Lucy Anderson using only papier-mâché, cotton cord, and hand painting.

Picture frames are among the many items that can be attractively decorated with papier-mâché techniques.

Jeanne Valentine Design, photographed at the Bazaar Sabado, Mexico City

Any round can from potato chips, soaps, waxes, etc., can be made into a work of art and used for desk accessories, umbrella holders, wastebaskets, flowers, anything.

Or a plain motel-type ice bucket can be beautifully redone with papier-mâché, lace trim, and hand painting. Cherries and leaf shapes are cardboard relief.

Round items photographed at Sala de Artes, Mexico City

Materials needed for decorating with predesigned papers are gift wrap or wallpaper, the object, scissors, and glue. For best adhesion, cover entire object with glue, then lightly cover back of paper. Work with a roller or brayer to ease out air bubbles. Open file box, Dona Meilach.

Covering with predesigned papers

Many people are timid about their ability to create designs. For you who lack confidence in your own artistic talents, do work with predesigned papers. You can cover entire objects using gift wrap or wallpaper simply by cutting the paper to shape and gluing it to the object. You may want to use contrasting papers for interiors of objects as shown in the assorted boxes and holders, above right. Black paper is used for the interior of the cylinder; checks and striped paper for the boxes. If your original containers lack covers or handles, you can make these from cardboard and papier-mâché, then cover them with the patterned paper also.

Using the patterned paper as your basis, you might add designs of string, then glaze all papers and strings as in the final step of any papier-mâché project.

Assorted items covered cleverly and beautifully with predesigned papers using the papier-mâché techniques.
Photographed at Sala de Artes, Mexico City

Zebra-striped paper is used on the outside of this umbrella stand which is combined with squares of papier-mâché used over the edge and on the inside.
Photographed at Sala de Artes, Mexico City

GIRAFFE. By Chicago public school children on exhibit at the Art Institute of Chicago. Illustrates the size project possible when the shape is built over an armature created from chicken wire and cardboard.

Courtesy, The Art Institute of Chicago

chapter 2

Papier-Mâché Over An Armature: Approach No. 2

The first approach shown for papier-mâché in Chapter One was to cover an *existing object* with papier-mâché, then redecorate it. In the second approach, papier-mâché is placed *over an armature specifically created to become the form* for the finished shape much as a human skeleton is the form of a person.

Armatures may be constructed from a variety of materials including special armature or hanger wire, screening, cardboard, paper-stuffed bags, boxes taped together, paper and cardboard tubes, balloons, malted milk cups, Styrofoam shapes, paper plates, molded aluminum foil, and any combinations that will result in the shape the artist visualizes. An armature enables you to create a shape as opposed to Approach No. 1 where the existing object dictates the shape. As a result, one can have a sculptural form that may be solid and bulky or airy and precariously balanced. Portions may jut out in gravity-defying directions.

Once the armature is made the procedures are the same as shown in Chapter One. 1) Cover the armature with papier-mâché; 2) seal; 3) decorate and reseal as necessary; and 4) paint and glaze.

Working with an armature is a challenge as you visualize how to build a skeletal form from the myriad unrelated materials at hand. Very small to huge examples can result and it is the method most often used for creating window displays, sculpture, and for classroom projects. Scope and size are limited only by one's imagination, materials available, and patience in developing large pieces.

Examples on the following pages are offered to stimulate possible uses to which you can put papier-mâché for expressive and decorative results. Additional applications of the armature approach are shown in Chapter Four for expressive sculpture, in Chapter Six for furniture and furnishings, and in work by and for children, Chapter Seven.

Armatures for papier-mâché are made from wire and combinations of other materials taped, pinned, wired, or papier-mâchéd together. There are U-shaped pins to hold unwieldy shapes of plastic foam together. Paper and plastic cups, cones from wrapping twine, cardboard tubes from waxed paper, toweling, etc., chicken wire, stuffed paper bags, balloons, and crushed aluminum foil make excellent armatures for all or parts of a form to be papier-mâchéd. Cardboard can be shaped and taped together as a basis for figures and sculptural forms. You can buy ready-made heads in many sizes from craft and hobby shops.

TORITO. A small bull made for use in a fiesta is thirty-two inches high and created of papier-mâché over a bamboo frame. You can discern the wood strips crossed over beneath the covering. Often, this bull is worn by a dancer and carried through the streets during the fiesta. This same principle may be used for making costumes for Halloween and other holidays and for stage productions.

Collection and photo: William E. Ward, Cleveland, Ohio

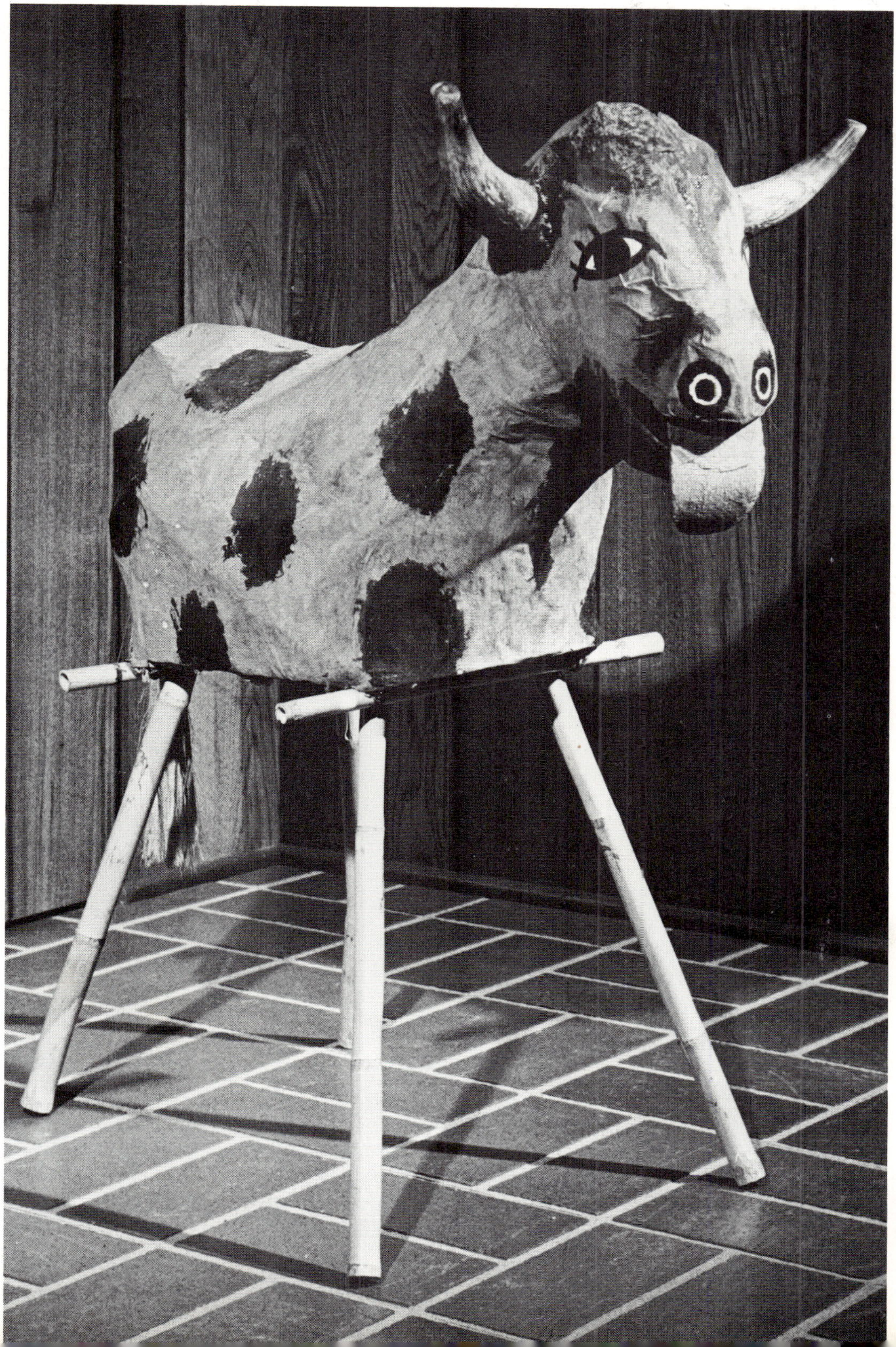

CANDLE HOLDER AND NAPKIN HOLDER. Phyllis Peterson. The candle holder is a plastic cup base with papier-mâché petals (made from layers of newspaper in the same way as the flower petals on page 26) arranged and glued to the cup. Napkin holder is made from one and one-half malted milk containers and a Styrofoam ball held together with long strips of glued paper, sealed, then decorated and painted.
Courtesy, Illinois Bronze Paint Co.

Use a whole malted milk container for the base, a half for the top with a Styrofoam ball for the head. Hold together with a strip of glued paper or with masking tape, then continue to place strips of papier-mâché over the entire piece.

Seal, then decorate with lace, paper trim, doily borders, etc. Hand paint details, antique, and glaze.

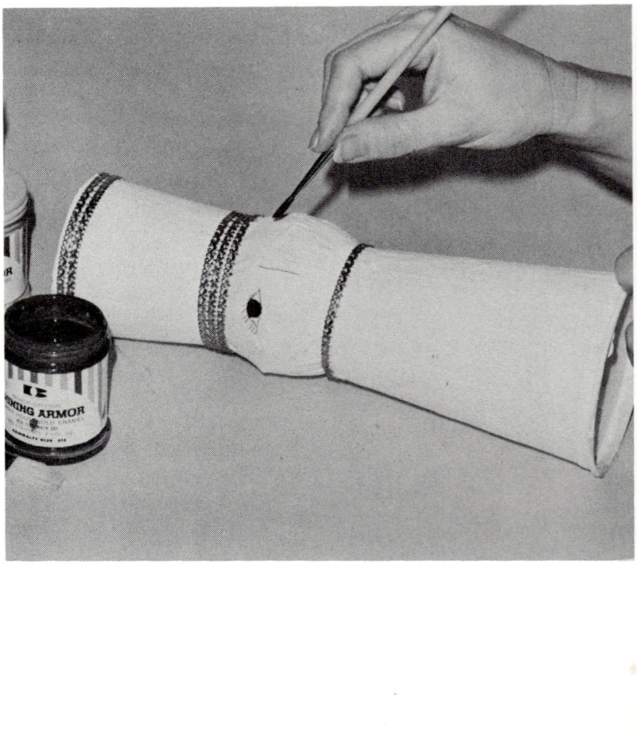

Different branches of owl families are created by Bob Lee from cardboard rolled to shape and held together with tape. Eyes are also made from cardboard. Paper toweling is used to create a rough texture, then the entire piece is hand painted, using matte finish designer's gouache. Parts are cut out so owls may be used to hold leaves, feathers, or flowers.

There's an old wives' tale that little girls are made of sugar and spice and everything nice, but Bob Lee's little girls are made of cardboard, tin cans, masking tape, and paint. Very often their heads are made from oatmeal boxes cut apart and perched on a cone of cardboard or Styrofoam. Sometimes their dresses have big holes in them so they may hold a spray of leaves.

Materials needed to make little girls might be a paper cup, tin can, cones from twine, paper toweling, cardboard, masking tape, glue, and paper towels.

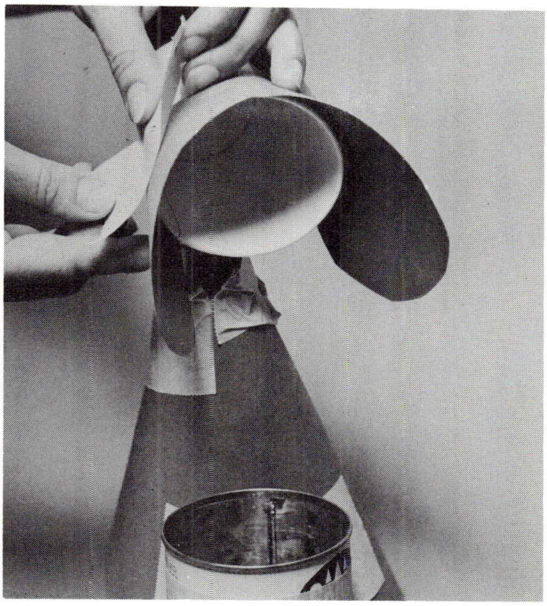

By combining parts imaginatively and taping together, you can make these whimsical maidens.

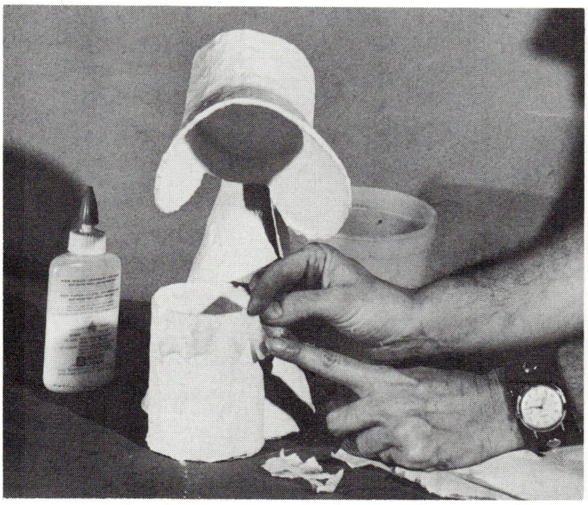

More paper toweling may be added in sheets or in small squares to build up edges if desired.

>

Here she is all put together and sealed with gesso over the paper toweling mâché that creates a texture. She's all ready to be decorated.

Build a whole city created from assorted sizes and shapes of boxes glued together, covered with papier-mâché, and painted. Steeples and odd shapes are cardboard or parts of boxes cut down, refolded, and decorated. ARCHITECTURE by Bob Lee.

Photo, Bob Lee

Hangers for the children's room, for guests, or for displays are also made from shapes of cardboard or wood, papier-mâchéd and decorated. All hangers by Bob Lee, Chicago.

MADONNA. Abelardo Ruiz. The form is composed of a Styrofoam cone body and a ball for the head; the "dress" and headpiece are formed from cardboard. The piece is papier-mâchéd, then painted in brilliant hot pinks, oranges, deep red, and golds with black outlining. It is highly glazed to a ceramiclike finish. A candle may be inserted in a holder in the headpiece.

Collection: Author

Rear view.

THE CONCERTGOER. Bob Lee. Papier-mâché forms may be dressed in real fabrics. This cardboard form, papier-mâchéd, is given a dress of lace, a coat of paper and fabric trimmed with ostrich feathers. Fabrics are used here as external dress and not dipped in glue. Front.

Rear view.

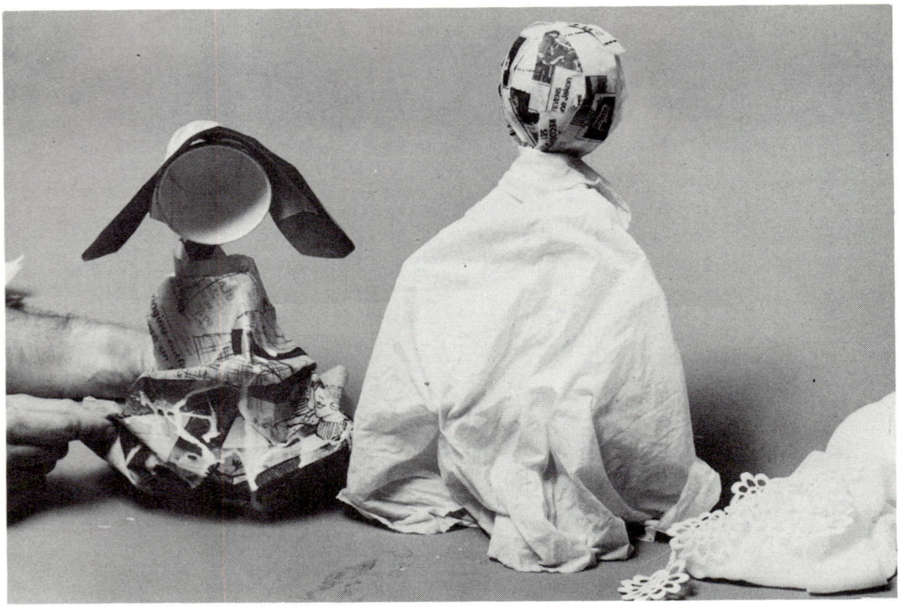

Paper and cloth dipped in glue create draped forms. Laces and other trims dipped in glue become extremely hard and permanent, often look like fine filigree china.

Drapery treatments with paper and fabric

The effect of drapery may be achieved with both paper and fabrics dipped in glue. Both harden to a solid material. At left, newsprint dipped in glue can be folded and draped. As the glue hardens it stiffens the paper. It is brittle when dry and can break; although if two or three layers of paper are added to the original drapery, it is very permanent.

Rags, cheesecloth, lace, and other thin fabrics respond beautifully to draping when they are first immersed in undiluted white glue. They can be used for the basis of the form and then decorated with papers and fabric trims. Textured, loosely woven materials such as curtains, burlap, chiffon, etc., may be added over a papier-mâché form for additional surface texture. Glue-wet fabrics should be propped or held until glue sets slightly and fabrics assume desired shapes. Dry thoroughly. Because there is abundant glue in the fabrics, it isn't necessary to seal the material unless there is a print that must be obliterated. Paint or glaze directly on the hardened, dried fabric.

Often the print of a fabric can become a finished portion of a papier-mâché piece. Rather than hand paint tiny detailed flowers on the apron of a peasant dress, Gemma's tiny print fabric became the apron shape of one of her famous figures (page 110). Varnish and other glazes may be used on glued fabrics as with paper.

Clowns of papier-mâché by Sergius are simply cones for a body, with rolled paper for arms. Feet and head are shaped of paper pulp. The "draped" costume is actually paper dipped in glue and folded, resulting in a hollow area between cone and drape portion. Lace around collar and cuffs is as stiff as ceramic. "Hair" is molded from paper pulp. Instruments are cut and formed from cardboard.

Angel is made of papier-mâché and covered with velvet for a Christmas display. It could also be used for a table centerpiece.

TO MARKET. Drapery arranged to look as though the wind is blowing.

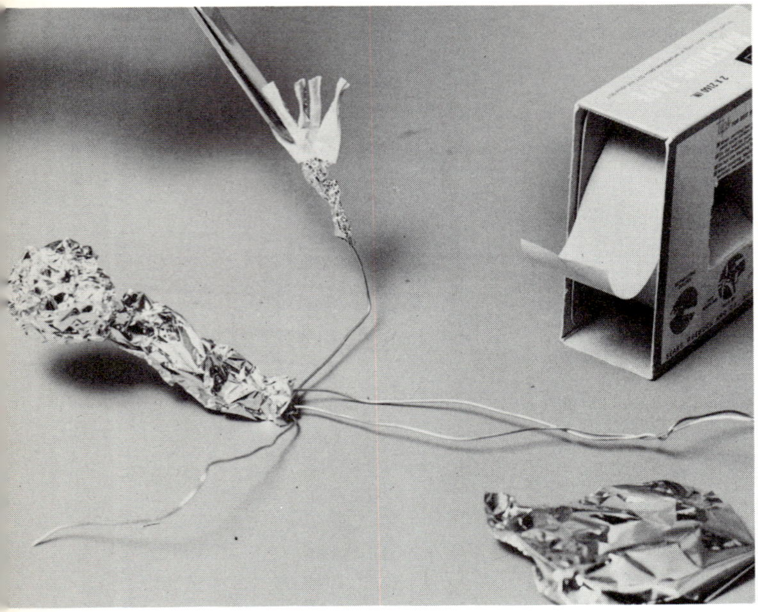

Soft wire sold by sculpture material suppliers for making armatures is easy to bend. Aluminum foil is molded around the wire to fill out the form and to create the fingers, etc.

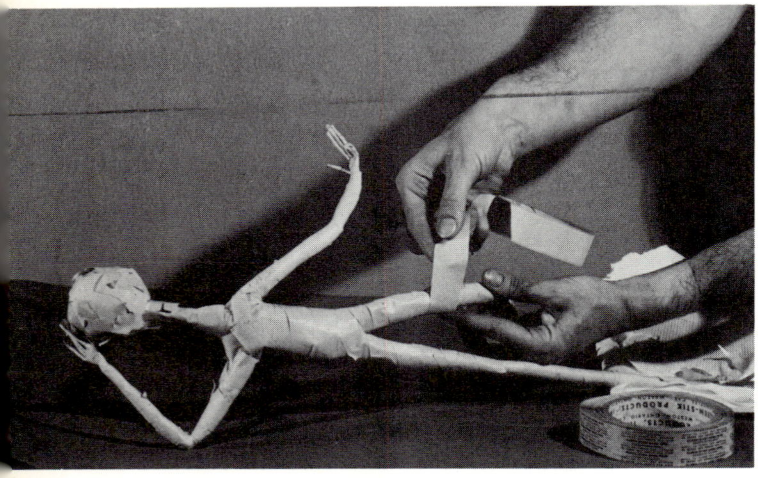

The form is further built up by wrapping the foil and wire with masking tape.

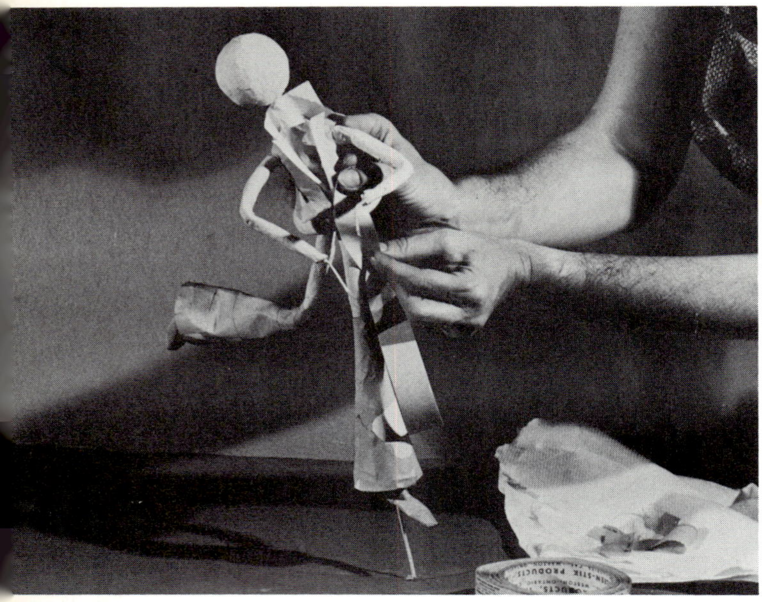

It is given a lightweight cardboard collar and pants which are covered with paper toweling.

The result is the Ice Skater . . . still in the process of being painted by Bob Lee.

Using the same technique, the figure might become a bride. By Bob Lee.

A trio of skeletons might play deadly tunes for the annual Mexican FESTIVAL OF THE DEAD. Skeletons, portrayed living a full and happy life, are made of wire armatures covered with papier-mâché and, sometimes, plaster.

THE ROADRUNNER. Eileen Bernard. Gesture and motion may be captured with wire and papier-mâché.

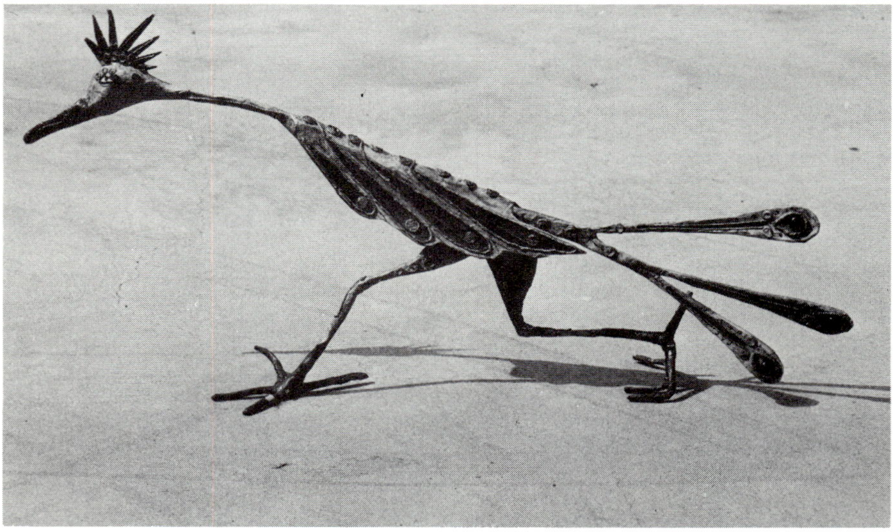

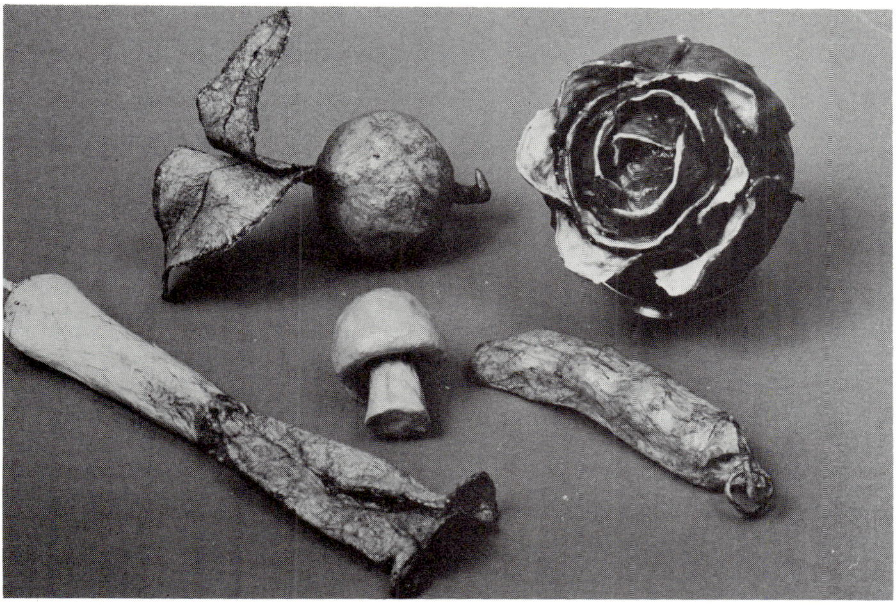

Vegetables (and fruit, too) are often made of papier-mâché over a form worked to duplicate food shapes. The beet, for instance, is wrapped over a Styrofoam ball using layers of colorful tissue. The mushroom is made of paper pulp, and the cabbage began over a balloon. The onion and peapod are made from shaped aluminum foil (below).

Because aluminum foil is so malleable, it is marvelous for odd-shaped pieces to be finished by the papier-mâché technique. Pea shapes are made of balls of foil and the "shell" is simply a sheet of foil molded to shape with a piece of wire added for a stem. The foil is made opaque white by gluing a sheet of paper toweling over it. When dry, squares of green and yellow art tissue are overlaid; the colors of the wet tissue run and blend so no painting is required. The object is then glazed.

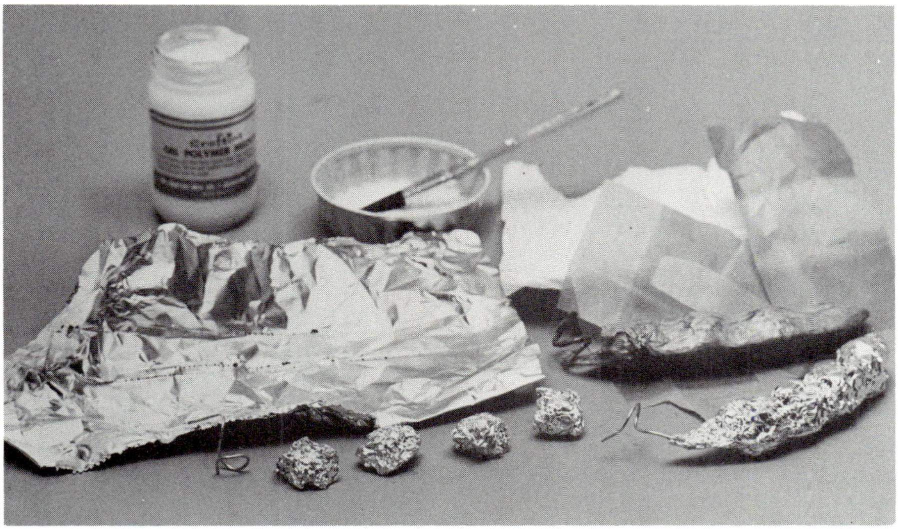

An armature may be created from many things. The object is to have it do the job. To make a dragon or monster such as those shown at right, simply apply ingenuity. Balloons are used for the head and body, rolled newspaper for the legs and arms, a bent roller from waxed paper for the neck. The mane is cut from lightweight cardboard, the tongue will be formed from rolled paper, the eyes and ears simply modeled with the wet paper as it is applied to the base form. Often you have to improvise, propping up the figure as you work.

Cut the cardboard and paper into tabs where it will attach to the balloons so it is easier to tape into place. After covering the form with papier-mâché, you can stick a pin into the balloons to break them, allowing the papier-mâché to dry from both inside and out. For added texture, glue a porous material such as curtain lace on cheesecloth on any area desired. Decorate and glaze.

The same kind of approach for developing armatures may be used for any form, real or fantastic, large or small. Dried gourds are excellent "skeletons" for odd body shapes, too.

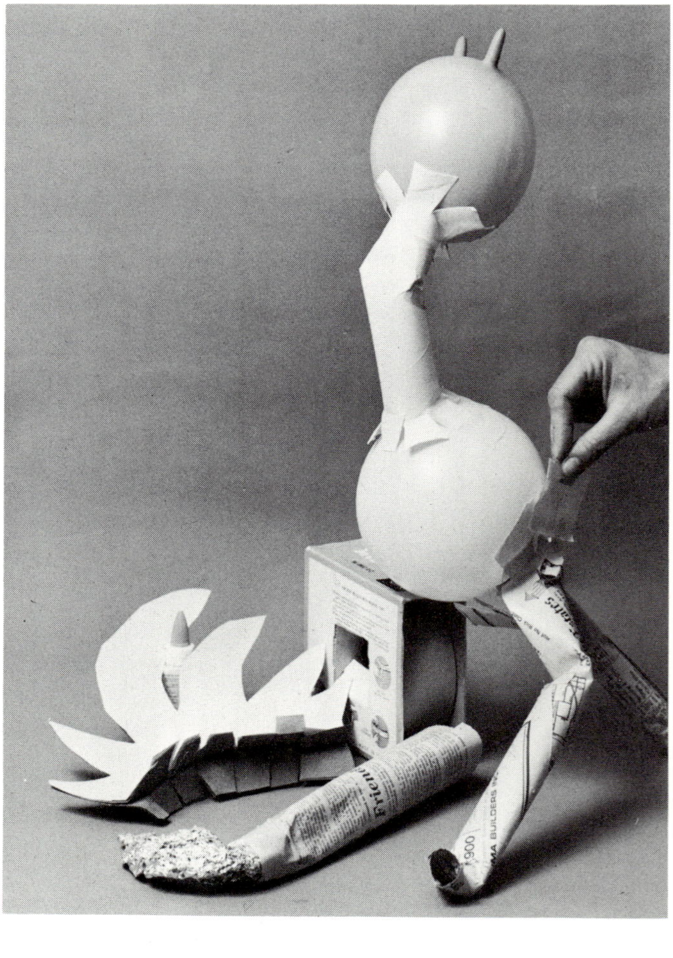

MONSTER. *Collection: Author*

DRAGON. *Collection: Ignacio Villaba y Mendoza, Mexico City*

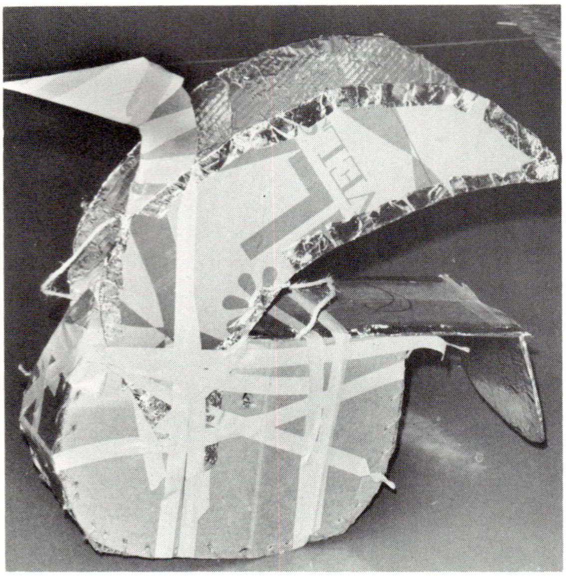

The well-known piñatas from Mexico, made to be filled with candy and later burst open, may be created over cardboard shapes held together by rope and masking tape. Edges are covered with aluminum foil to add glitter.

Tissue and colored foil paper are cut into fan shapes, rippled, and folded in half, then opened and pasted in an overlapping arrangement.

The entire form is covered in this manner.

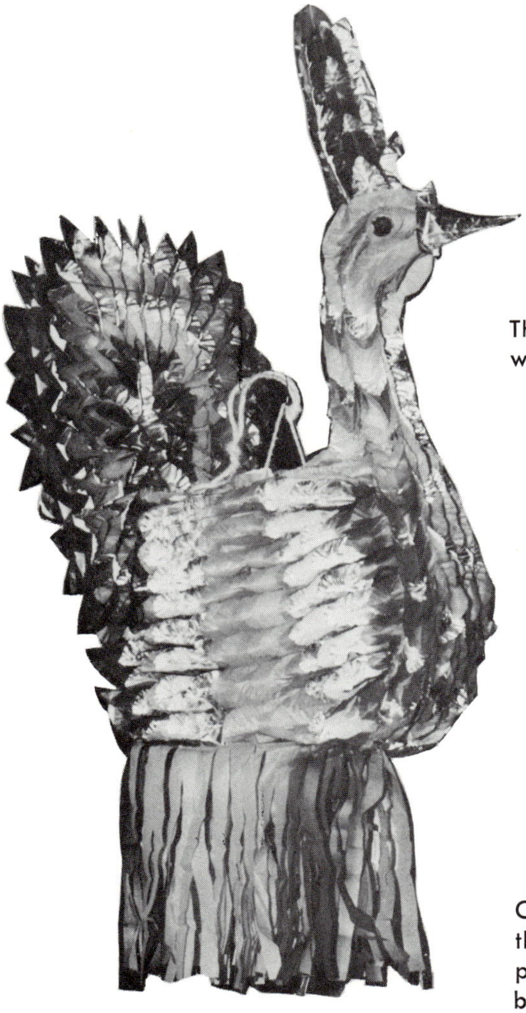

The result is a gay proud bird with a rich, colorful plumage.

Or a small bull from the bullfights that is a replica of a traditional piñata is made to be carried home by tourists.

Piñatas may also be made over rolled newspapers or over balloons. This horse and lovely little girl by Elizabeth Piest uses only rolled paper for armatures. They are covered with clipped strips of wrapping tissue glued on in layers and are great for parties or just for decoration.

Once you become aware of the armature concept, you can almost determine what probably was used for some shapes. For this horse wooden legs have been cut to form, then combined with chicken wire for the body.

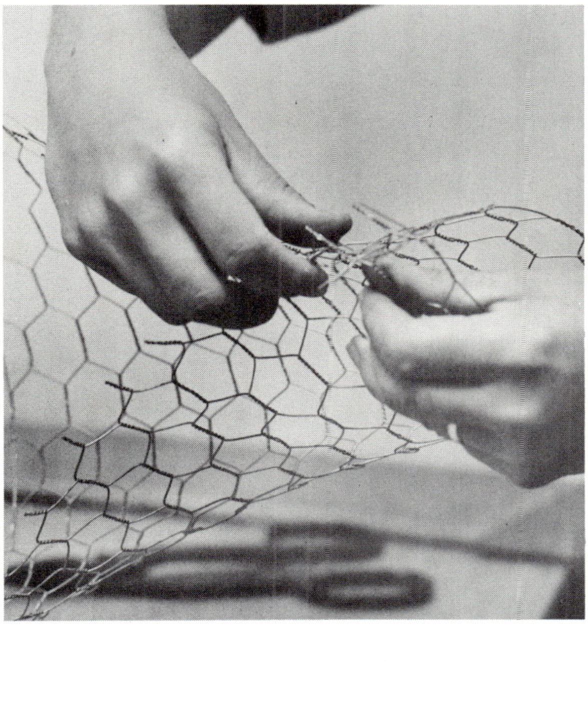

Chicken wire is easy to use. Cut a piece to the approximate shape you want with wire-cutting shears. To assemble, bend the straight wires around other wires curving the wire as you work. The wire can be squeezed and pulled out until the form is achieved. One shape may be wired to another or the wire may be combined with other materials such as wood, cardboard, paper, etc., for an infinite assortment of forms. (See page 118 for another chicken-wire demonstration.) Papier-mâché strips are applied in layers and in opposite directions to cover the wire. When dry, it may be sealed with gesso and covered with a thin coat of plaster for a smoother appearance.

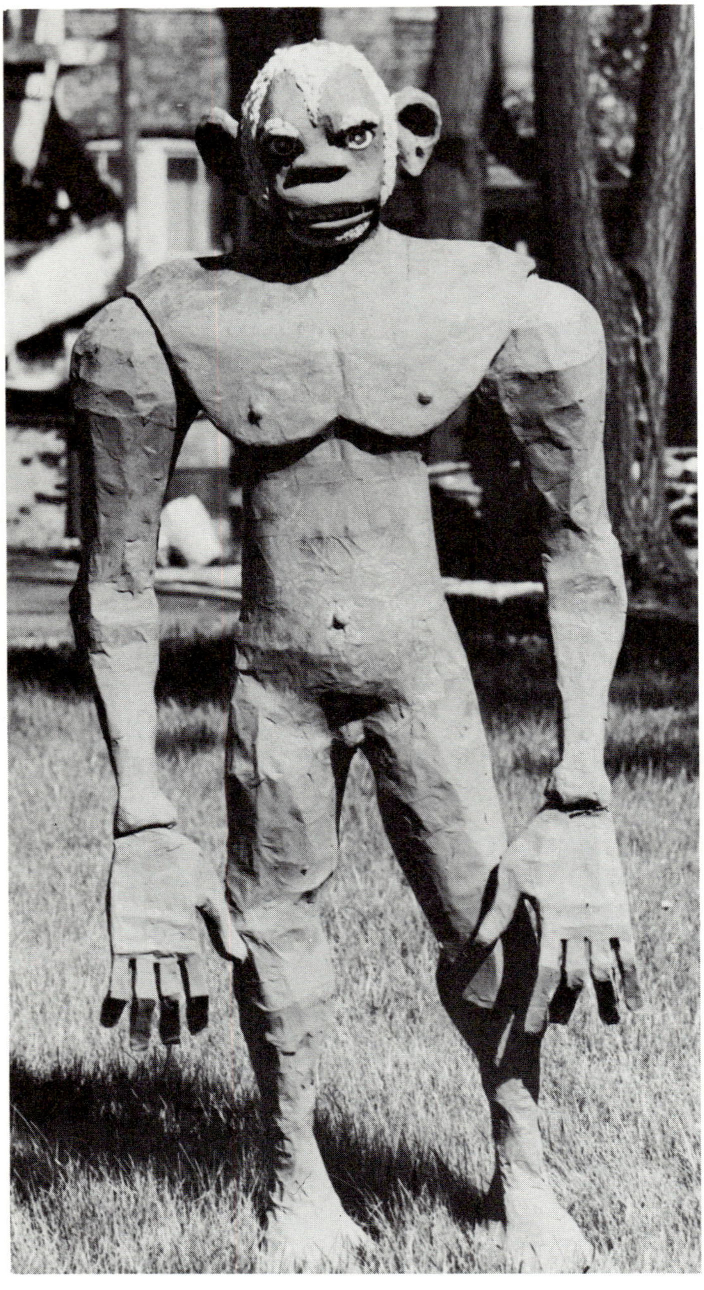

GORILLA. Samuel Sims. Made over chicken wire and cardboard. His arms are movable by the force of a small battery-operated motor accessible from the "door" in the back (see rear view below). Because papier-mâché is lightweight, movable parts are feasible.

Photographed at the Edward Sherbeyn Gallery, Chicago

PUPPETS. Bil Baird. The famous puppeteer relies heavily on all papier-mâché techniques for the heads of his various characters.

Courtesy, Bil Baird

chapter 3

Using a Mold for Papier-Mâché: Approach No. 3

The third approach for making a papier-mâché object is to work into or over an item that serves as a "mold." This means the item merely serves as a basis for a papier-mâché "casting" to be formed; when the mâché hardens, it is removed from the original mold. The cast mâché has the same shape as the mold: the mold may be used over and over again to make many duplicates.

A mold may be an object you have at home such as a bowl, a pot, a ceramic or silver dish, a piece of sculpture, a toy, a clay shape, a basket, almost any item you may wish to duplicate and still maintain the original in its perfect form.

The advantages of working from molds are that you can re-create a shape without permanently covering the original. You can combine shapes and remove the mâché even where shapes are thick in the middle and thin at the ends so the original will not slip out easily. You simply cut the papier-mâché form in half, remove the original and then tape the halves of the papier-mâché together again. Proceed, using the same steps described in Chapter One. Another advantage is that you can readily duplicate shapes if you have only one original. Should you want a pair of vases, for example, you can make a duplicate with papier-mâché. Should you wish to re-create a successful form for gifts or sales, the mold technique has that advantage.

Molds may be created by the clay-and-plaster-method demonstration beginning on page 96. One-piece molds may be used for plaques. Two-piece molds are usually made for three-dimensional shapes.

The following practices will simplify working from molds:

1) Always use a separating medium on the mold so the papier-mâché will not stick to the mold. This might be vaseline, a light coat of talc, a sheet of aluminum foil, nonstick sandwich wrap, or strips of wet newspaper (without glue).

A display of decorative papier-mâché pieces. Although items vary in hand decorating and color, shapes are duplicated by the mold method.

2) For the first coat of papier-mâché next to the original, use a paste solution that does not stick too hard such as flour and water or a thin solution of wheat paste without white glue. A layer of wet strips of paper without glue will also suffice. Aluminum foil or sandwich wrap will adhere to the papier-mâché but not to the object. If you want to conceal these separating materials cover with a layer of papier-mâché for a more finished appearance.

3) Exercise good judgment about placing papier-mâché over edges of a mold; always work so you can free the mold from the original with a sharp knife or a spatula. If the papier-mâché tears as it is removed, it can be easily patched with additional strips of papier-mâché or with masking tape that is then covered with more mâché strips.

4) After the original is removed and the papier-mâché form is patched, follow the same basic procedures for sealing, decorating, and finishing as shown in Chapter One.

The examples that follow were created from one or more objects used as a mold.

This will give you an idea of how to combine shapes from simple objects and how a mold works. A bowl and dish were used to make a sun hat. Grease outside of glass bowl lightly with vaseline and cover with two layers of papier-mâché strips overlapped on the outside of the bowl. Let dry several hours. Remove when papier-mâché is still slightly damp so you can manipulate crown to your head shape. Then dry thoroughly.

With the bowl removed, the crown of the hat remains. Now a dish is greased to serve as the mold for the "brim." The crown of the hat (now completely dry) is placed off center on the dish, and strips of paper are placed over the crown and dish until the dish is covered.

When the papers of the brim are dried, the dish is removed. Because of drying times required, papier-mâché items may require several days to complete.

The edge of the brim is trimmed and the hat is ready for decorating. Any variety of shapes may be created for costumes or for sunning, for table decorations, for hat blocks in a closet, etc.

A dried papier-mâché shell will easily come away from a bowl that is wider at the top than the bottom so the bowl can slip out. However, you may wish to re-create a shape that is wider in the middle and will not pull out of a mold normally. The beauty of papier-mâché is that you can cut the hard paper shell, remove it from the original, and then put it back together again. Dona Ziegler shows how it is done over a large rattan basket.

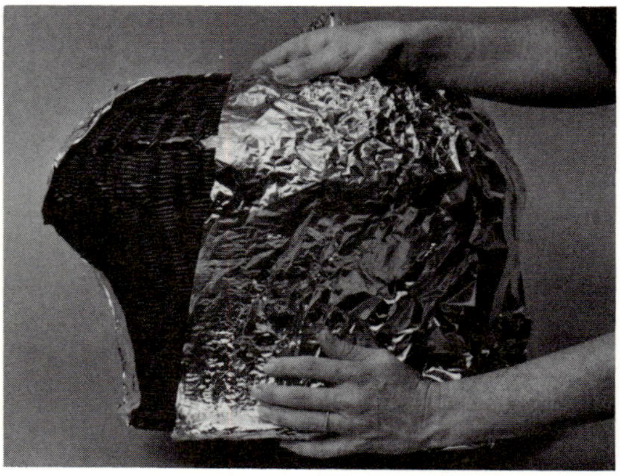

Cover the basket with aluminum foil which becomes the "separating" medium. Sandwich wrap (such as Saran) may also be used.

The outside and bottom of the basket are covered with three layers of papier-mâché strips overlapped both vertically and horizontally.

The basket completely papier-mâchéd. Here, the top rim is covered also as the paper will be cut from the basket and the finished piece will have a rounded edge. Because the foil is used, the papier-mâché does not adhere to the basket. Dry thoroughly.

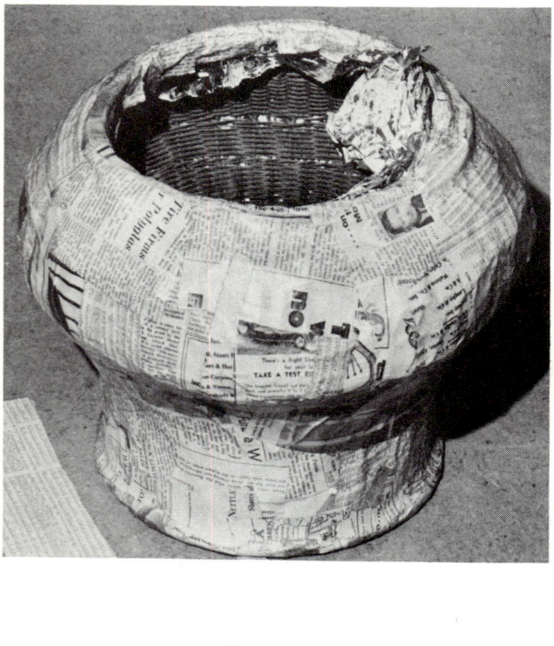

When dry, cut the papier-mâché in half, including the aluminum foil, and remove from the basket. Use masking tape and put papier-mâché halves together: cover entire shape with another layer of papier-mâché. (If other areas tear, simply tape and cover.) Seal with gesso and decorate.

SKELETON HEAD. Fred and Barbara Meiers. Sculpture inspired by Mexico's "Feast of the Dead."
Photographed at The Egg & The Eye Gallery, Los Angeles

ACCESSORIES. Jeanne Valentine Designs. Papier-mâché over existing objects. *Photographed at Los Castillo, Mexico City*

FLOWER GIRL. Bob Lee. Papier-mâché over cardboard cones and cylinders taped together.

ANIMALS. David Gilhooly. Papier-mâché over formed chicken wire armatures. *Photo, courtesy, artist*

SCULPTURE. Martin Serrano. Smooth and textured finishes.

CENTERPIECE AND SNACK SERVICE. Lucy Anderson. One silver dish was the mold to duplicate the snack dishes. The centerpiece was molded over a toy drum.

PATIO TABLE. With modern paints and finishes, glued-paper designs over an old iron table may be protected from varying weather conditions.

Photographed at Sala de Artes, Mexico City

ROG ORANGUTANG. David Gilhooly. Chicken wire was shaped to form the animal, then covered with paper strips and instant mâché to create the outer "skin."

Photo, courtesy, artist

BASKET LADY. Dona Ziegler. The basket is decorated using the same procedures as in Chapter One.

Collection: Mr. & Mrs. Nicolas Plotnikoff, Lake Bluff, Illinois

Rear view of above.

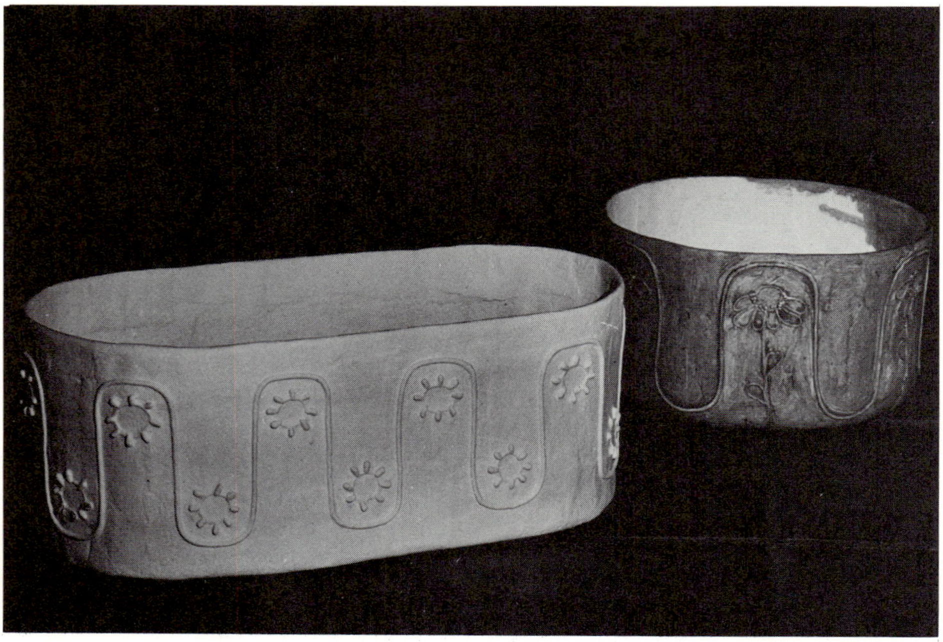

It is easy to identify the molds used when you see pieces in their sealed stage. Lucy Anderson used a large roasting pan for her mold to create the unusual pot (left). A copper planter served as the mold for the pot (right).

Two different-sized bowls served as molds for the footed dish (left), one used right side up, the other upside down, and then the two taped together to create one dish. (Front) A covered jewelry box was the mold used. For the lampshade, an egg carton became the base for the papier-mâché (not used as a mold). Lucy Anderson.

Two bowls, one inverted on the other, were the molds for this vase (left). The vase (right) was made from a jug used for the mold. The papier-mâché was cut in half, the jug removed and the halves taped together as in the demonstration on preceding page. Lucy Anderson.

Finished objects that duplicate cans, dishes, jars, and pots. The small flower holder (left) was molded from a cylindrical can for the bottom and an inverted dish for the top part. Feel free to use only portions of objects as molds. The bowl of a stemmed glass may be used upside down for a lid, but only apply the papier-mâché over the bowl and top of stem. Other covers are made of cardboard with handles of molded papier-mâché or wood. Lucy Anderson.

If you need a large flower holder for a centerpiece, you might use a mold from a large pot, half of a china crock, or even a child's drum. Cover any of these with foil or sandwich wraps. Papier-mâché, then remove the dried paper shell from the object. The small trays for serving appetizers were formed over an original silver candy dish. Handles were added made from rolled pieces of cardboard. Lucy Anderson.

One dish, upside down, was the mold for the turtle's shell, his head, legs, and tail were added with paper pulp. A smaller dish was the mold for the flower carrier on his back. Lucy Anderson.

A hanging flowerpot. Lucy Anderson. The backing was cut from cardboard. A large flowerpot was covered with mâché, then cut in half and only one half used for this planter. The other half was used to create a "pair."

One flowerpot used as a mold was made into a large planter by inverting one form on top of the center. Note that the top pot was made without a "bottom" so it could become the hole for the dried flower arrangement. Lucy Anderson.

Once the object is completed, it is often difficult to determine whether the mold was the shape of the finished item or a combination of a couple of shapes. Lucy Anderson has put together two bowls perfectly and with enough layers of paper so the seam does not show.

Papier-mâché fruit may be made by the same "cut in half" technique as the bowl. Cover or grease a piece of fruit, cover with papier-mâché. Dry. Cut the mâché in half, remove the fruit and tape or mâché the halves of the papier-mâché piece together, then seal and decorate. Dorothy Courtney.

Re-create an animal from a clay model you make yourself or from a plastic toy. For a clay model, use plasteline clay that already has a wax base so water-base glue will not adhere to it. If the form is plastic, grease or cover with foil. Then papier-mâché, dry, and cut the mâché in half, removing the original. Decorate as desired. Elephant by Frances Gove.

For this mushroom group, Frances Gove used pieces of cardboard tubes for stems: the rounded form is made over an electric light bulb. When dry, the bulb is removed and the top glued to the stem.

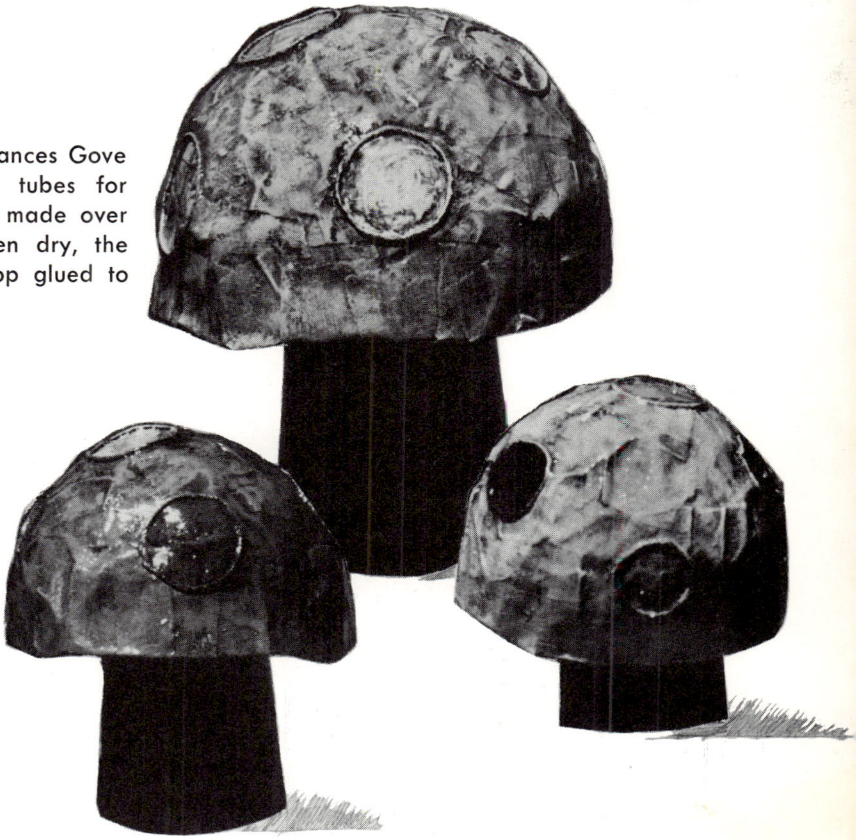

Gemma Taccogna is shown with some of the papier-mâché figures for which she is famous. The figures were originally made from clay, then two-piece molds poured of the clay models. Usually front and back are separate molds. The cut papier-mâché halves are taped together at the side seams. Details and painting are added by hand. For a ceramic finish use six coats of sealer and two coats of undiluted white glue for white parts. A color glaze is made by mixing about an ounce of white glue with four ounces of temperas. A final glaze of lacquer or varnish is added for protection.

Courtesy, Gemma
Photo, Jim Schumacher

The plaster mold

Working into or over bowls, over clay forms, toys, and other objects will yield an unending assortment of shapes and combinations of shapes. However, there will be situations when a more complex shape is desired. Often, one will want several of them. The most efficient way of reproducing papier-mâché pieces is with a mold made from plaster. Use plaster of Paris available in hardware stores, or casting plaster from art and ceramic suppliers.

Industrially papier-mâché is made from plaster molds. Many craftsmen, finding a ready market for their handmade pieces through local art-craft and gift shops, will discover that making plaster molds can expedite their output, yet still retain the label of a handmade article. A plaster mold is also an excellent project for art students. They discover that the basic mold technique is applicable to many art media in addition to papier-mâché. The same mold can be filled with clay, wax, and molten metals when it is properly prepared.

To make a mold you must first create a form from clay. Plasteline clay already has an oil base so the plaster will separate from it easily. (Because plasteline has an oil base, it does not harden readily and may be used over and over.) Pottery clays can be used if they are available, but they should be stored in plastic bags to prevent hardening.

The clay form should be fairly simple without any undercuts so the papier-mâché "casting" will pull easily away from the mold when it is dry. The plaster mold may be filled with either paper pulp (instant mâché), with squares, or strips.

Molds may be made in one or more parts. In the demonstration, a one-piece mold is shown. Normally, a one-piece mold will produce "half" a shape, that is: the back of the finished casting will be either *flat* if paper pulp is crushed in or *open* if strips are used. The result will be more like a plaque than a three-dimensional piece to be viewed from all around. However, if the form is such that two halves can be made and taped together, one can achieve a three-dimensional shape from a one-piece mold. But remember, because the cast is always the reverse of the mold, it must be designed so the two halves will be compatible when placed together.

For a fully three-dimensional casting, one needs a "two-piece" mold. These are made in the same way as the flat mold, only with a separator between the two halves so the plaster will become two opposite sides of the original as in the following examples.

Papier-mâché molds are used to create duplicates of Jeanne Valentine's creations in her studio and workshop in San Miguel Allende, Mexico. At right, a clay kangaroo is being created for a possible new form. These are considered "two-piece molds" with the front and back of one object separated. After the mâché is placed in the mold, dried, and removed, front and back are put together.

>

Margit Cohen uses the two-piece mold to create heads for her dolls. She fills the mold with paper pulp, or instant mâché, for a solid shape rather than a shell. Heads are sanded and covered with several coats of sealer and lacquer for a smooth finish. Dolls © Margit Cohen.

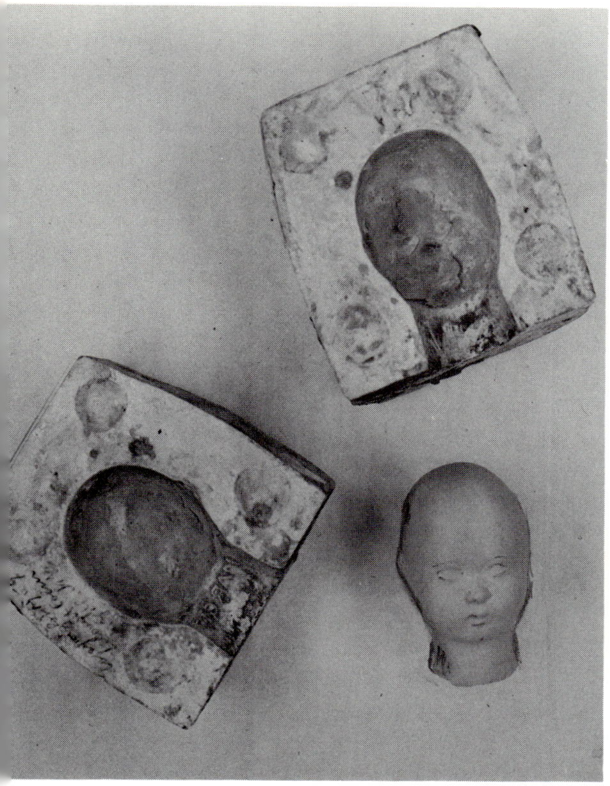

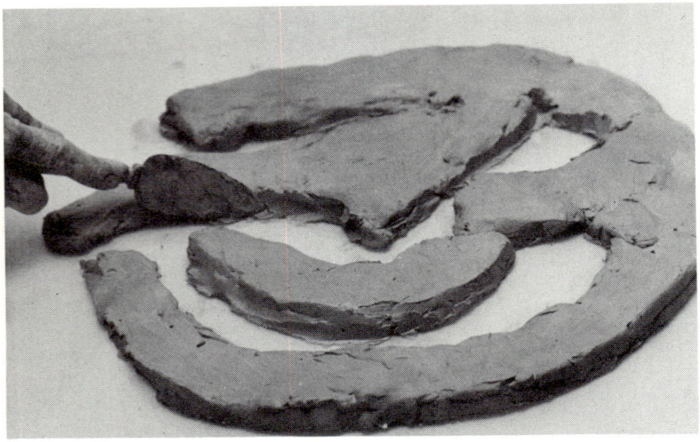

HOW TO MAKE A PLASTER MOLD

1. The original is designed in plasteline clay. Work on a flat surface such as a piece of glass, a dish, or a plaster batten. Work the clay with a flat knife and a wet sponge until the desired shape and smoothness are achieved.

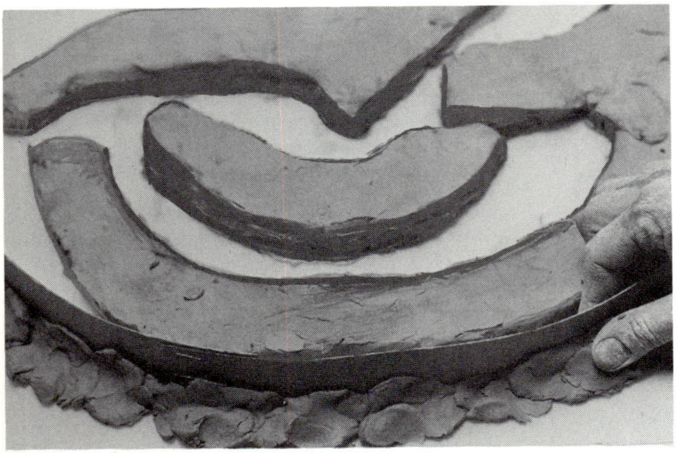

2. The shape must be "walled" to contain the plaster. Here, strips of cardboard are placed around the form and held up by pieces of clay. The cardboard's inner surface is greased with vaseline so it will pull away from the hardened plaster.

3. Mix plaster according to directions, always adding the powder to the water gradually and stirring gently with a spatula from the bottom up to make sure all lumps are incorporated and mixed. Tap the bowl gently so all air bubbles come to top. Plaster should be about the consistency of sour cream: thick enough to hold without being runny, not so thick that it sets too fast.

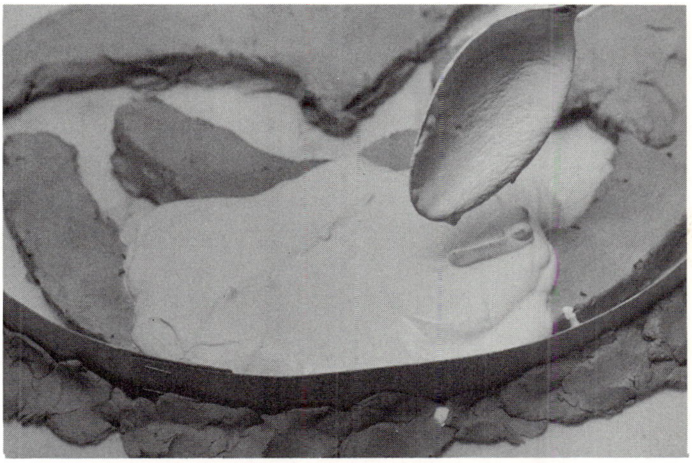

4. Spoon and pour the plaster over the clay until the whole form is completely covered with a layer of plaster at least ½ inch thick.

5. When dry, remove the cardboard and the top of the mold will look like this.

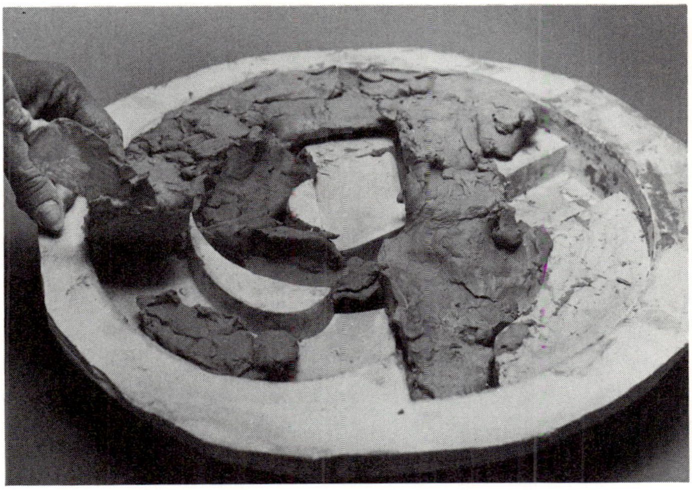

6. Turn over and remove the clay. The result is a negative form of your original clay model.

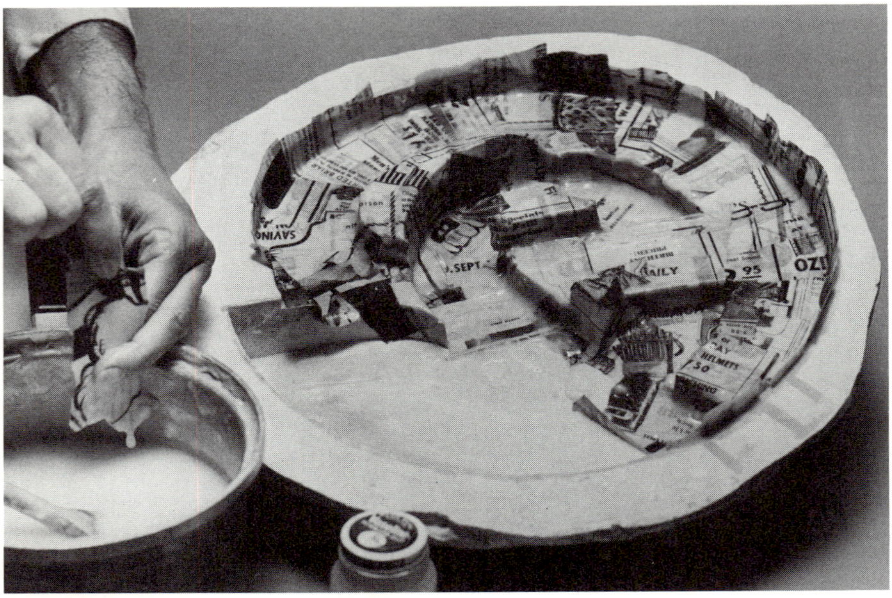

7. Grease the inside of the plaster mold thoroughly with vaseline or other separating medium, removing excess grease with a tissue or towel, and begin to lay in strips of newsprint. Use flour and water for the first layer because it doesn't stick as hard as wheat paste and white glue. Use wheat paste and white glue for subsequent layers. Experiments showed that when the first layer was glued with white glue, it was very difficult to remove from the mold even though a separating medium had been applied. Build up three layers and, for convenience, use different parts of the newspaper for each layer, for example: want ads for one layer, news and display ads for a second layer, and the colored graphic section for the third.

8. Brush a coat of undiluted white glue over the third layer for extra strength. Dry the paper thoroughly before removing from mold. It will dry more rapidly if placed in the sun or in a gas oven overnight. Do not turn on the oven; the heat generated from the pilot light will be sufficient.

Carefully remove the form from the mold, using a spatula at the edges if necessary. Should the form rip, mend with tape and additional layers of papier-mâché.

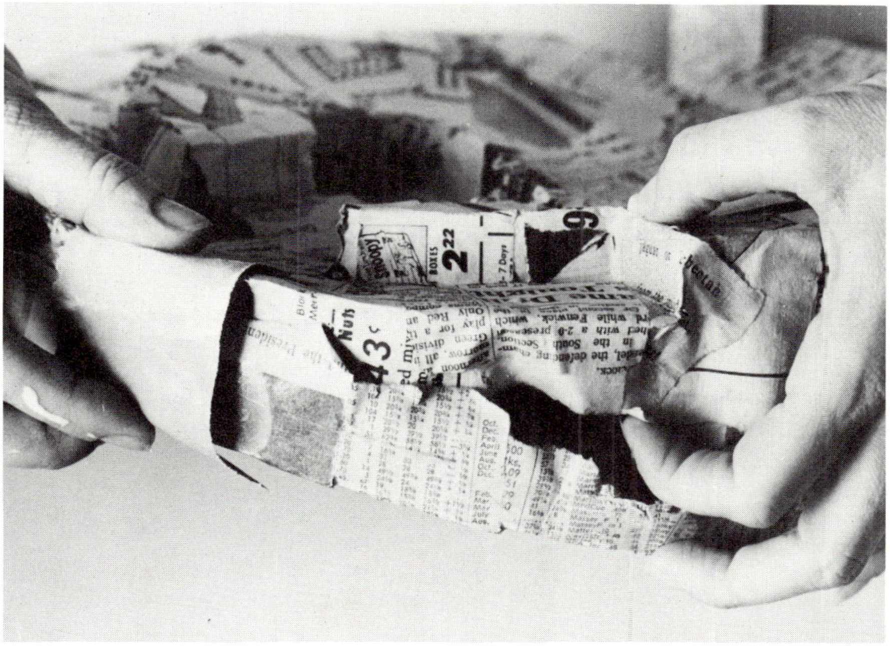

9. For a plaque, trim the edges and attach plaque to a piece of cardboard or wood. Mâché sides and back together for a more finished appearance. Seal and paint. Or make two halves of the mold and place together with mâché or masking tape. Repaper over the masking tape to create the same radial design of the pasted papers. The entire piece is sealed with gesso.

10. Then the piece is painted and finished. This hanging is different on each side and painted with Daz-L and black stripes for a glowing effect under black light. It may be hung as a mobile. Dona Meilach.

Musicians are made from a one-piece mold and used as plaques. By Jeanne Valentine.

Photographed at Los Castillo, Mexico City

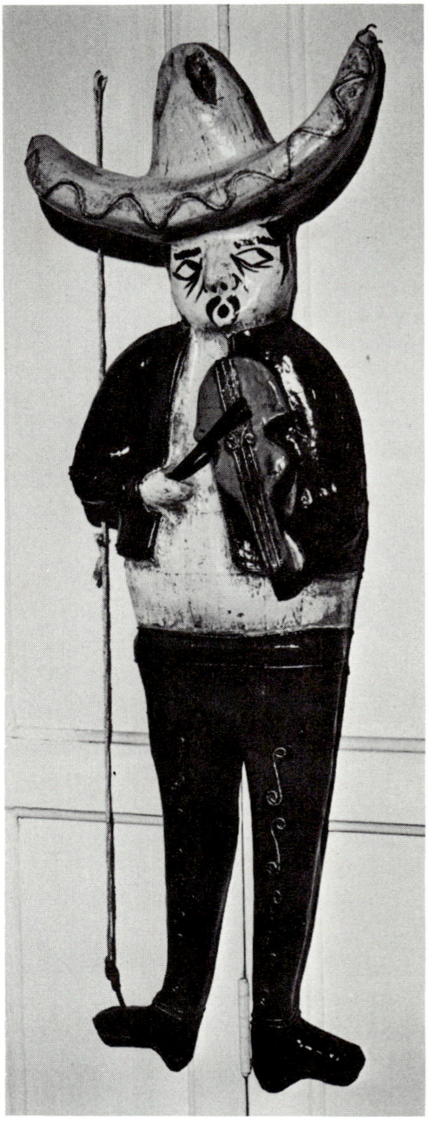

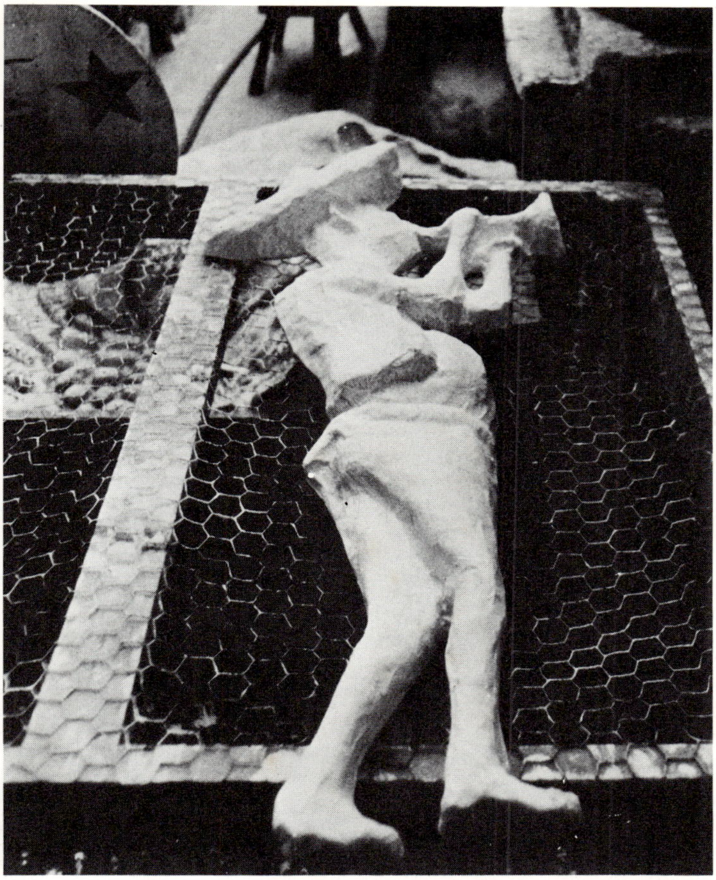

To dry large pieces, set them on racks made from wire mesh so the air can circulate freely all around.
Courtesy, Jeanne Valentine

A partially finished owl plaque is set back in its mold to demonstrate how it was formed. The feet and ears are three dimensional so a two-piece mold was used only over those portions.
Courtesy, Jeanne Valentine

The elephant in the throes of creation. It is sealed with several coats of primer.

The finished, hand-decorated elephant. Jeanne Valentine design.

Photographed at Los Castillo, Mexico City

Turtle candy dishes made from molds.

They are tied together to prevent warping and to make sure lids will fit properly.

Photos, Courtesy Jeanne Valentine

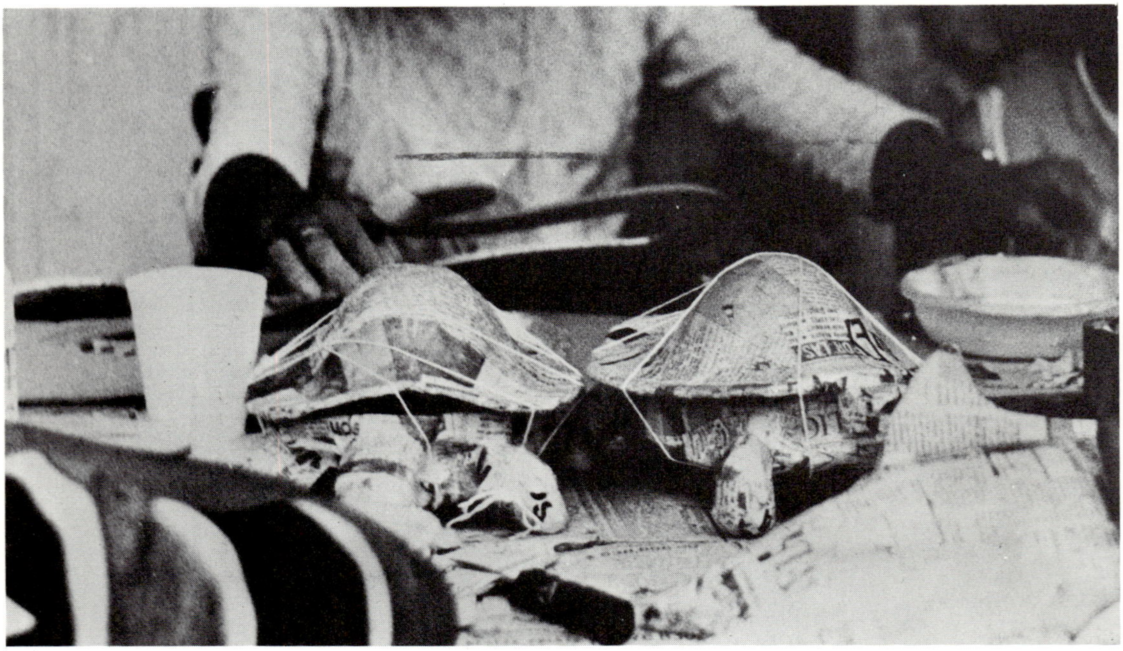

CAT. Jeanne Valentine.
Photographed at Los Castillo, Mexico City

To achieve finer details, a papier-mâché form may be covered with several thick coats of gesso or with plaster: texture is created in this coating. Gemma adds texture with a comblike plaster tool to create striations on a surface before it is painted.

Courtesy, Gemma
Photo, Jim Schumacher

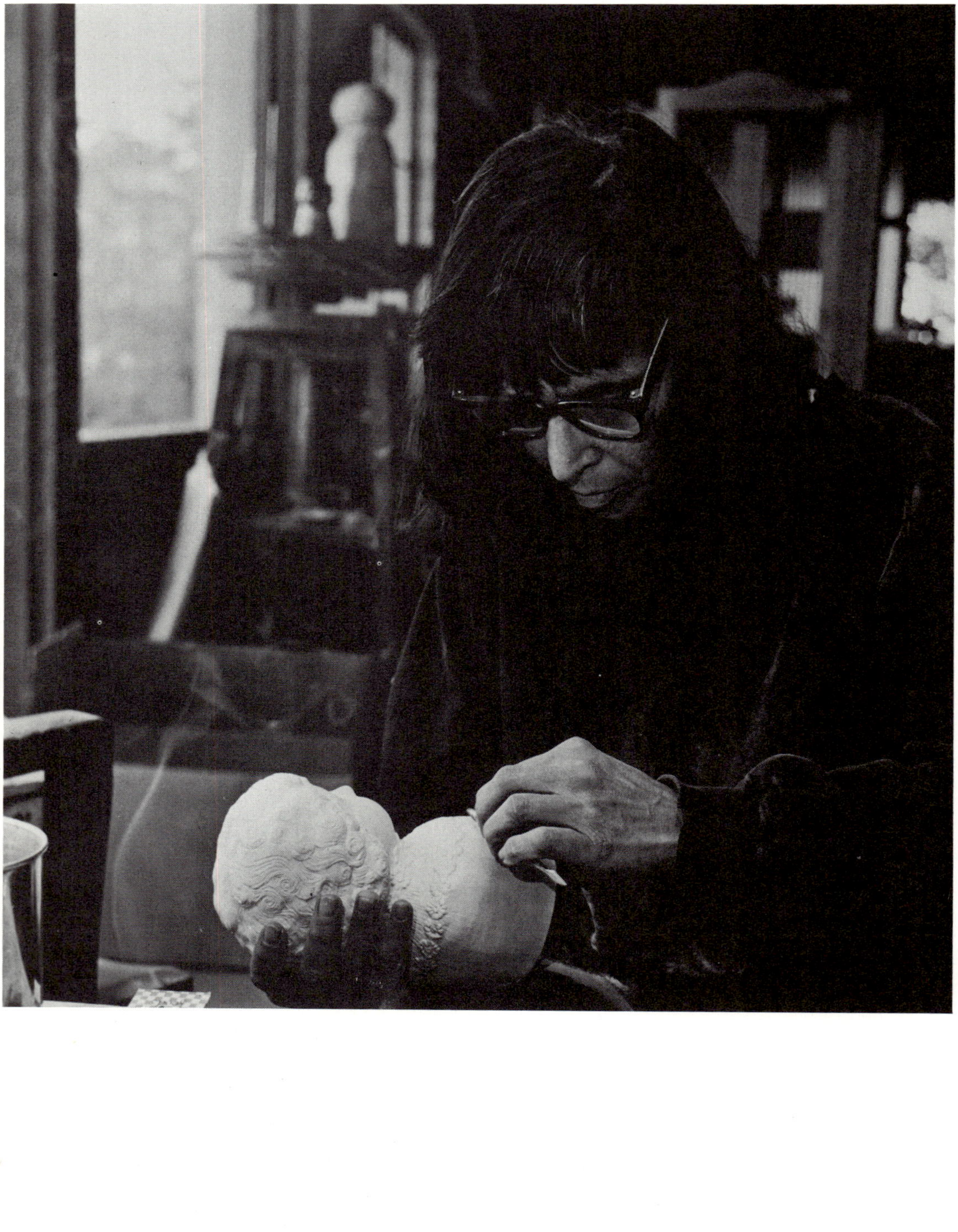

After the papier-mâché is pulled from the mold, it must be put together with additional papier-mâché or tape and the paper worked along the original lines of the mold.

Courtesy, Gemma
Photo, Jim Schumacher

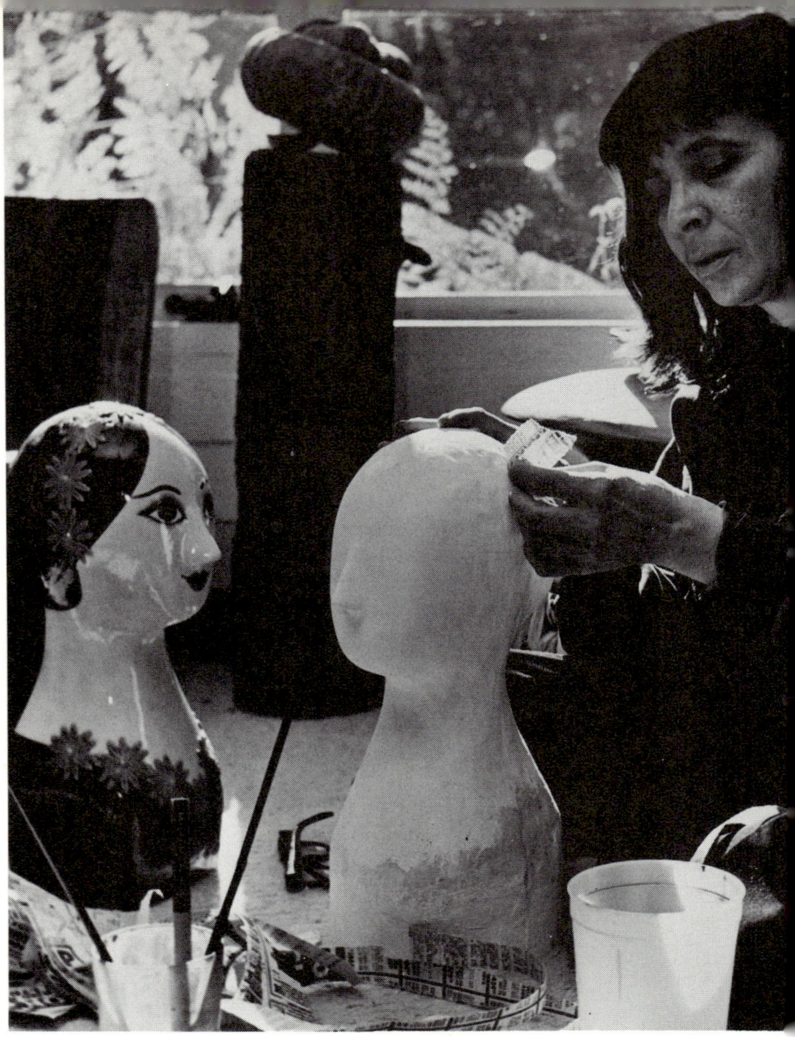

Even after a piece is sealed, additional paper may be added to revise a shape.

Courtesy, Gemma
Photo, Jim Schumacher

Or after the form is removed from the mold, the pattern of "squares" may be added to the front.

Courtesy, Jeanne Valentine

Gemma is shown with several of the head shapes she has created.

Courtesy, Gemma
Photo, Jim Schumacher

Actual pieces of lace are added to the dress for a raised surface texture.

Courtesy, Gemma
Photo, Jim Schumacher

After this lovely lady was painted, her apron was added; it's a piece of printed fabric which is covered with the glazes. "It's a great idea for those who don't feel they are so talented with drawing," says Gemma.

Courtesy, Gemma Photo, Jim Schumacher

Intricately decorated animals are a creation of Jeanne Valentine. Tails are added from solid shapes of paper pulp over a wire and covered with squares of papier-mâché.

Photographed at Los Castillo, Mexico City

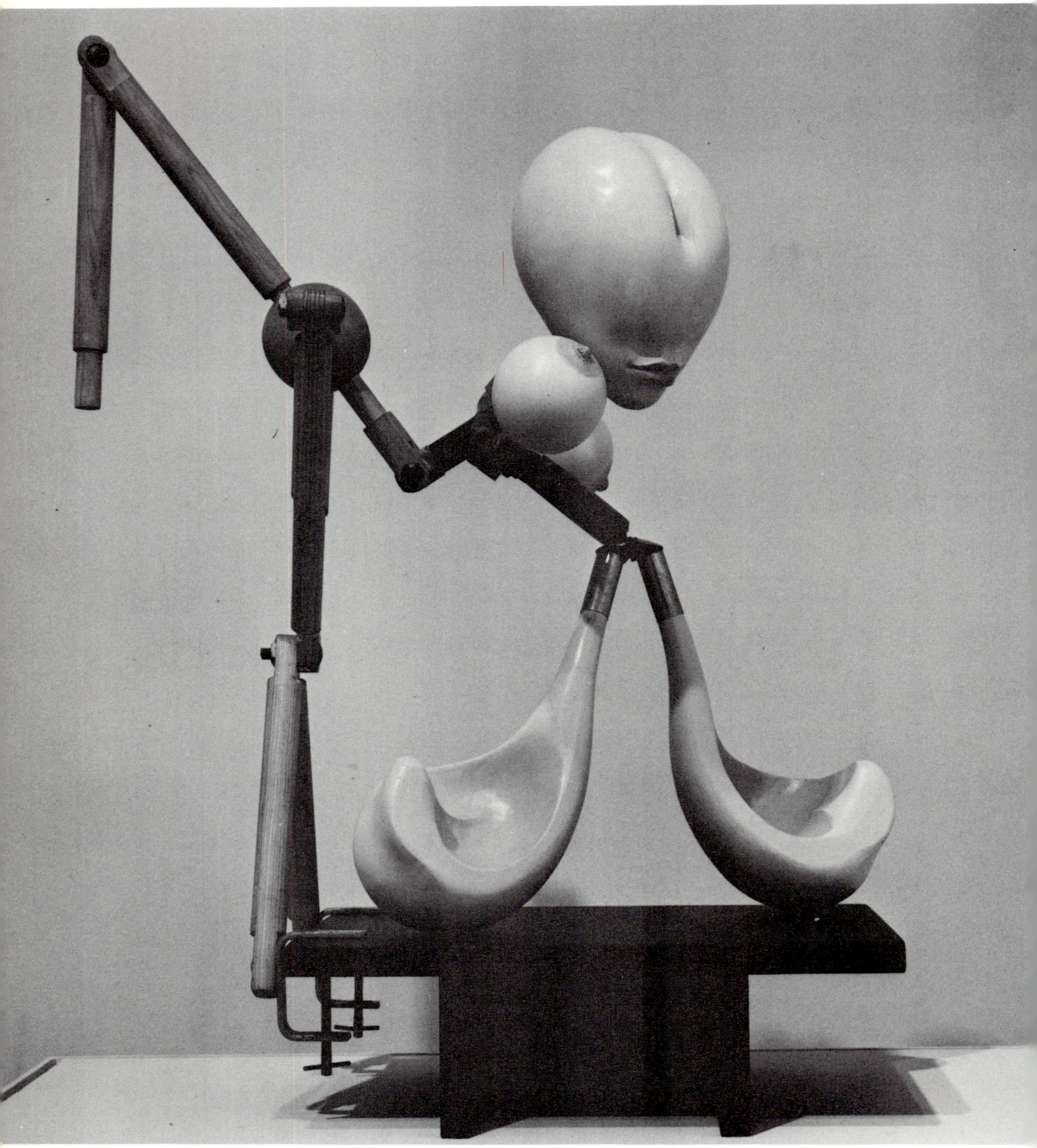

MACHINE-GUNNERESS IN A STATE OF GRACE. Hans Bellmer. 1937. Wood and papier-mâché.

Collection: The Museum of Modern Art, New York

Part Two STIMULATING IDEAS FOR PAPIER-MÂCHÉ

chapter 4

Papier-Mâché for Expressive Sculpture

Traditionally, papier-mâché has been associated with decorative and applied arts. In contemporary art-craft circles, it has rarely been considered a permanent medium for the serious artist. Perhaps this is because it has been a material used in the schools as artists have grown up; so they tend to think of it as an "exercise" medium. Schoolroom papier-mâché, rarely given a permanent finish, has proven to be fragile and easily breakable. And more sophisticated finishes are usually not part of a school art department's budget. So, artists, bent on having a lasting work for their efforts, leaned toward more permanent materials for their serious works.

In the last few years, however, papier-mâché sculptures have appeared in museums and art galleries and private collections. With polyurethanes, alkyds, polymers, and other chemical achievements, the versatility and potential permanence of papier-mâché are being rediscovered by many artists. It is inexpensive to produce, easily portable and, should a sculpture be damaged en route to a showing, it is easier to repair than a stone or wood sculpture. Papier-mâché sculptures can be made extremely colorful, showy, and weather resistant, thereby presenting great advantages for the outdoor exhibitor.

The techniques used to create a sculpture are no different from those presented in Chapters One and Two. Only the ideas differ, often having satirical and symbolic messages. Most often, forms are made over armatures such as chicken wire bent and shaped, or over combinations of shaped and taped-together boxes. A thin coat of plaster may be applied over the gesso coat for a better painting surface and one that can be built up and textured in infinite ways. The potential of papier-mâché in combination with other media is also being explored.

>

VIVIAN. Niki de Saint-Phalle, 1965. This hulking shape is deceptively light-weight because of its papier-mâché medium over a wire form. Despite its feeling of solidity, it balances precariously, gracefully on one foot. Its surface decoration consists of yarn, painted designs, fabric scraps, and textured paper. To work on a form such as this it may be propped and strung with ropes as shown in the demonstration . . . page 118.

Collection and Courtesy, Joseph Randall Shapiro, Oak Park, Illinois

PERSONNAGE AU FOND ROUGE. Jean Dubuffet. 1954. Newsprint used as flat collage actually is a variation of the use of papier-mâché. Here it is combined with ink drawing.

Collection and Courtesy, Joseph Randall Shapiro, Oak Park, Illinois

ORGANIC FORM. Martin Serrano. Sculpture—two views. Various textures, colors, shapes, and finishes are possible with papier-mâché. Observe the contrast of rough and smooth, convex and concave, dark and light, glazed, antiqued, and enamel finishes that all work together in one beautifully articulated sculpture.

TISSUE DISPENSER. Decorate a plain wood or plastic tissue holder with papier-mâché to customize matching vanity accessories.

SCREEN. Jeanne Valentine. Panels of cardboard, wood, or Masonite may be covered with papier-mâché and hand painted.

Photographed at Los Castillo, Mexico City

MASK FROM TAIWAN. Heads such as this may be made from papier-mâché to be used for theatrical production, costumes, and sculpture.

Photographed from the Collection, Field Museum of Natural History, Chicago

BASKET. Dona Ziegler. A large rattan basket can serve as the mold for several finished papier-mâché pieces that resemble fine porcelain when painted and glazed.

Courtesy, Illinois Bronze Paint Co., Lake Zurich, Illinois

JEWELRY BOX. Thin paper squares and paint give an ordinary, old chest a new personality.

CASTLE. Myrna Greenberg. Cardboard boxes assembled form the basis for this architectural wonder. It is covered with papier-mâché and bas-relief designs and decorated with lace beads, doilies, colored acetate for windows, and other materials.

THE EMBRACE. Miguel Angel Gonzalez. This individually sculptured piece has a personal expressiveness that is also universal.

DUET. Miguel Angel Gonzalez. Papier-mâché is deftly combined with drawing.

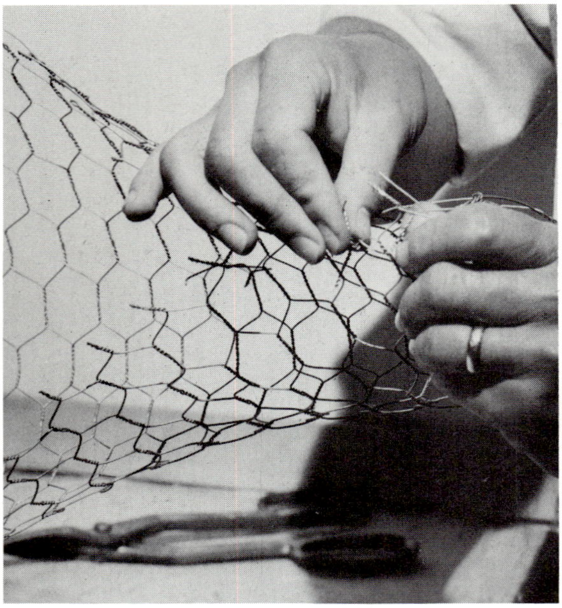

Working with chicken wire is essentially the same for all objects, varying only in the solutions to specific construction problems. Using the ends of the cut hexagons, wind the wires to make desired forms. Chicken wire can be squeezed, molded, and rebent until the form is achieved. A wire cutter and pliers are handy.

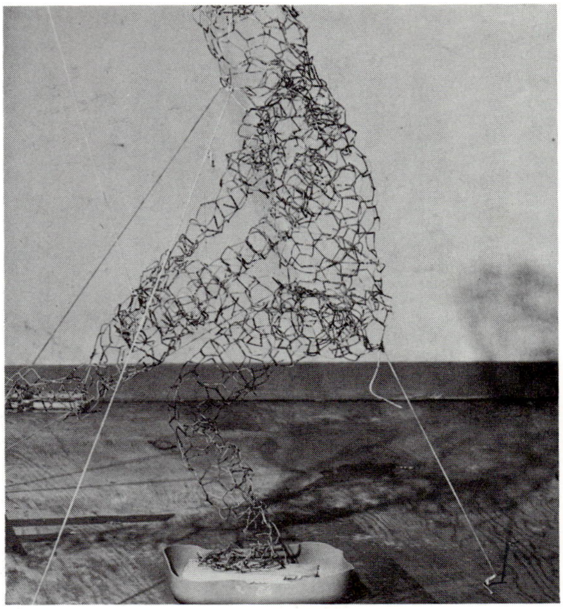

Forms that are to be balanced on one foot may be suspended by a series of ropes tightened tautly around staples or nails hammered into workbench and trussed around hooks or pipes on a ceiling, depending upon the working area. One foot is nailed to a block of wood set into the bottom from a plastic bleach bottle. Plaster will be poured into this form to make a solid, heavy base.

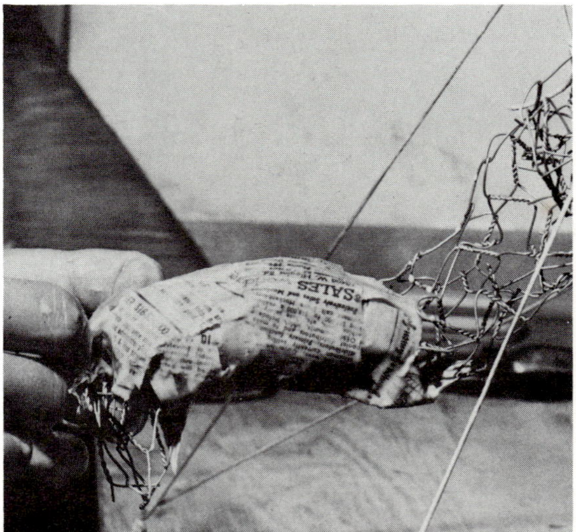

Then simply begin to overlap layers of newspaper strips until the entire wire skeleton is covered. Strips should be placed first in one direction, the second layer in another direction for greater strength. It is also easier to determine how many layers are being used when directions alternate.

THE SHOPPER. Florence Deeley, 5 feet tall. Made completely of papier-mâché over a chicken-wire foundation. The base was a box top from laundry soap filled with plaster for weight. After papier-mâché strips were dry, a thin coat of plaster was used for the sealer.

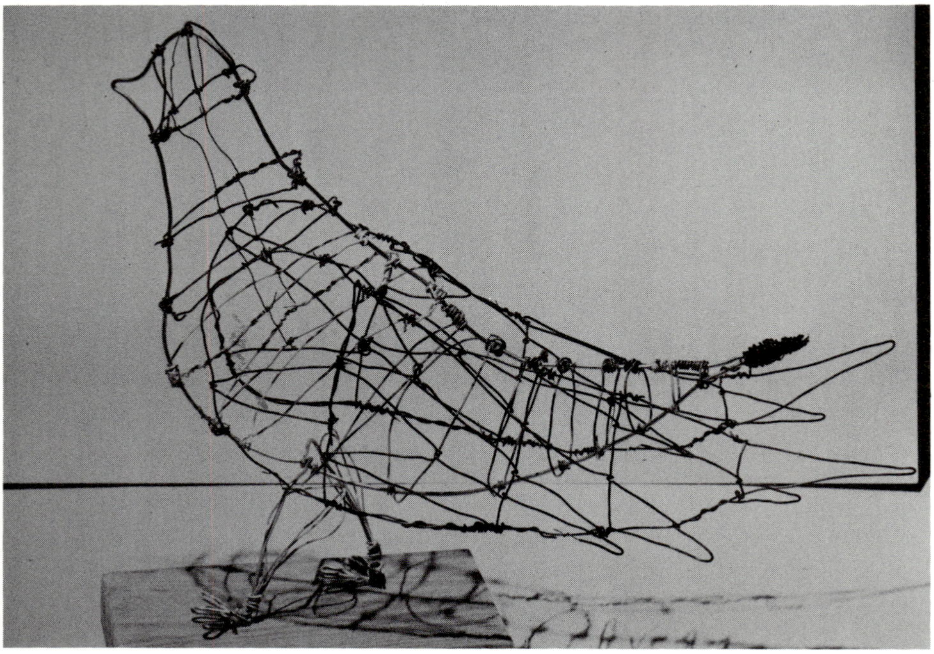

Open wire sculptures are also possible by using easy-to-bend armatures or any other lightweight wire that can be shaped and wound into a skeletal structure. Stiff hanger wire is used for the heavy outlining, then lighter weight armature wire used to develop the rounded body.

The piece may be completely covered with various papers in both solid and transparent sections.

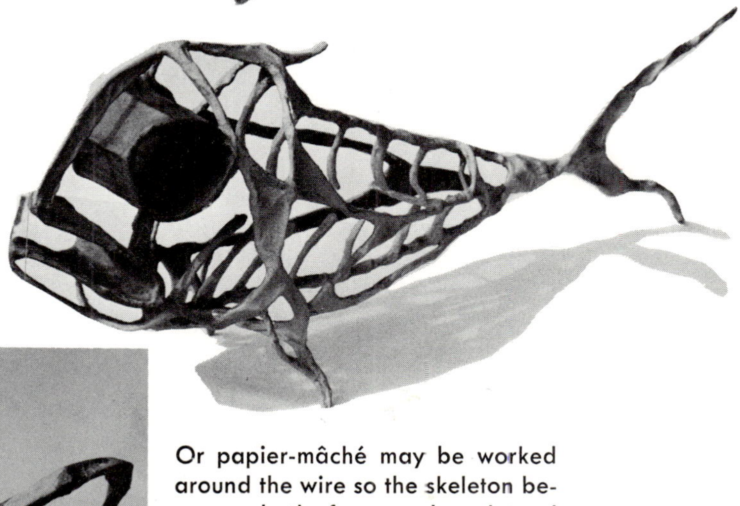

Or papier-mâché may be worked around the wire so the skeleton becomes both form and sculptural expression. Animals by Phyllis Satz.

WALLACE. Gerald Scarfe. Life-size papier-mâché sculpture catches the gestures and caricature style in a three-dimensional work.

Courtesy, Waddell Gallery, New York
Photo, John D. Schiff

HUMPHREY. Gerald Scarfe. 1968.
Courtesy, Waddell Gallery, New York
Photo, John D. Schiff

NIXON. Gerald Scarfe. 1968. These sculptures of political figures illustrate the easy adaptability of papier-mâché for use as satire.

Courtesy, Waddell Gallery, New York
Photo, The Sunday Times, *London*

ROCKEFELLER. Gerald Scarfe. 1968.
Life size.

Courtesy, Waddell Gallery, New York
Rockefeller Collection

ROY MANDRILL. David Gilhooly. 1969. 4 feet high. Life-size animals are made over chicken-wire forms, then developed using instant papier-mâché, paper strips, textured papers, and watercolors.

Photo, Mary Auvil

HARRY AND FAWN GELADA BABOON. David Gilhooly. 45″ high and 39″ high. Chicken-wire form with instant papier-mâché, textured papers, and watercolors.

Photo, Mary Auvil

CHRIS SLOTH. David Gilhooly. 3 feet long. *Photo, Mary Auvil*

CHAIR. Roger Baird. Papier-mâché with fabrics and fur pelts added to simulate figure. Chair decorated with printed papers and hand painting.

Courtesy, Crocker Art Gallery, Sacramento, California
Photo, Barbara Herberholz

HOT DOGS. Linda Cross. Each 8″ long. An expression of pop art using papier-mâché over Styrofoam "buns."

Courtesy, Artist

QUEEN OF HEARTS. Jan Miller. Cigar box, cardboard, and foam ball are used for an armature.

CONFORMITY. Jan Miller. Made over egg cartons.

Papier-mâché figures are marvelously adaptable to theatrical work. They are lightweight, can be created to any scale, and used for a progression of expressions and emotions where the script calls for specific nuances. Clothing may be changed; heads may be made interchangeable so the same figure may be given varying poses and moods. Stagecraft studio workshop.

Photo, Courtesy, Gemma Taccogna

Finished figures "on stage" with live actors and actresses.

Photo, Courtesy, Gemma Taccogna

chapter 5

Papier-Mâché for Decorative Plaques

Among the many popular uses for the decorative techniques of papier-mâché is a wide assortment of plaques. They are fun and easy to make. The results can yield scores of compliments and provide a feeling of accomplishment even among those people who profess "no artistic talent."

The examples of plaques shown are offered to stimulate your own creative talents into individual designs. There are plaques that can repeat the appearance of the outside of your home, those made for children's rooms, many that look like fine collages and oil paintings.

As with decorating papier-mâché boxes, armatures, molded items, the same principles illustrated in Chapters One and Two apply; this is simply another idea for creating beautiful things from papier-mâché. Plaques may be framed. If not framed, the papier-mâché should be brought around to the back of mounting board for a smoother finish. Plaques may be edged with fringe or ribbon depending on the effect you wish to create.

Generally, you will want to work on a backing of a piece of wood, masonite, or canvas board that will not warp. From there, you can build up layers of paper, shapes of cardboard, add glue-dipped fabrics and paper toweling, seal the surfaces, then hand paint, antique, and glaze as desired. Plaques may also be made from molds as shown in Chapter Three. They are especially effective where duplicates are desired for pairs.

For plaque ideas, use photos from magazines, advertisements for foods, Christmas and toy catalogs, children's books, and other attractive illustrations. One may design from pictures completely, or use photos as an inspiration for making your own individual tastes. Draw or trace outlines on board, work with papier-mâché relief shapes, seal, paint, and glaze.

THE APPLE TREE. Dona Ziegler. A piece of ¾-inch pine has been covered with squares of papier-mâché. A tree shape was outlined with heavy string, then filled in with lighter twine worked to simulate tree bark and coated with heavy paint and glaze. The apples and leaves are made of shirt cardboard glued to the surface, then hand painted. All string and cardboard were glued, dried thoroughly, then the entire plaque sealed with gesso, dried, hand painted, antiqued, and glazed.

Collection: Mr. & Mrs. Kenneth Benjamin, Lake Bluff, Illinois

For the "Honeytime" plaque (right) an entire board is covered with strips of newsprint which form a pattern of rectangles. When the front is dry, the back is also covered for a more finished appearance.

To form the beehive, undiluted white glue is spread on the area to be covered (lightly outlined in pencil), then cotton clothesline is worked back and forth. Cardboard leaves and bees are pasted on. The entire surface is gessoed to seal. When dry the board is sprayed or hand painted a background color. Details are hand painted. Surface is antiqued, allowed to dry, then glazed with a coating of polyurethane or varnish.

HONEYTIME. Dona Ziegler.

Series, Courtesy, Illinois Bronze Paint Co.
Photos, Warren Meyer

PORTRAIT. Irene Nelson. If you have an old frame, cut a wood or cardboard backing to fit, then make a portrait of someone you know using the plaque build-up method of drawing with string. Cover the backboard with papier-mâché, sketch in design, and build up. Where a smooth ceramiclike surface is desired such as on the face, cover with two or more coats of gesso and a coat of straight white glue, allowing each coat to dry thoroughly. Tint and finish with a high-gloss product.

FLOWER. Irene Nelson. Make a garden for your wall that will last all winter. You might repeat a motif from wallpaper or from a bouquet. Buds are built up by folding paper, saturating with glue to hold to board and to hold shape.

NAVIGATOR AND COLUMBIA. Irene Nelson. Backing is of masonite. Squiggles at top are formed with pottery clay (plasteline clay will not d-y beneath paper) coated with white glue, then covered with paper strips. Figures are "drawn" with string.

CARDBOARD RELIEF PLAQUES. Merrily Ickes. Created using the same procedures as decorating papier-mâché objects. The principle (shown at right) is to build up several layers of cardboard so some are high, some low for a greater tactile quality and more visual interest.

Courtesy, Illinois Bronze Paint Co.
Photos, Warren Meyer

1. Cut an overall shape from cardboard and glue to wood backing, using ½-inch to ¾-inch pine. Cut smaller shapes from shirt cardboard, tagboard, cereal or dress boxes and overlap and build up several layers. Cut the overall shape first, then continue to build up in layers.

2. Add string dipped in glue for fence details. Allow glued areas to dry thoroughly, coat entire board with gesso to seal. Dry.

3. Paint entire board one background color with either spray or brush-on paints. Always spray with object upright set into a box to confine spray. Dry.

4. Hand paint details. When dry, antique lightly, then use a final glaze coat as desired. Put a hook on the back, hang and enjoy.

NAPOLEON. Susan Meilach. Created from relief technique using lightweight cardboard in built-up shapes, then painted and glazed.

MERMAID. Susan Meilach. Cardboard and papier-mâché.

NOAH'S ARK. Dona Ziegler. Blocks with relief figures mounted on a papier-mâchéd backboard. String used for outlining.

TIGER IN THE CROCUS. Dona Ziegler. Two blocks of wood are glued to a larger block. Papier-mâché is on the relief blocks. Drawing on the backing board creates the "forest."

LITTLE GIRL. Irene Nelson. Notice that the squares of papier-mâché are put on in a radiating fashion for a design in keeping with the overall oval shape. Construction paper gives a heavier overlap at edges than newspaper.

MOUSE-COOKERY. Phyllis Peterson. Overlapped newsprint strips radiate as the outer design. The glazed inner oval is created by brushing the board with three coats of gesso, then two coats of straight white glue. The design is hand drawn and painted. The border is made of thinned plaster squirted through a cookie decorating tube.

THE GENERAL. Irene Nelson.

QUEEN ISABELLA. Irene Nelson. The Queen's ruff is modeled from glue-dipped sheeting. The braid and hair are made of heavy rope braided and glued. Features and face are hand painted. String is also designed and glued to the frame to complete the presentation.

HUTCH. Mura Bright. This chest might easily be created by someone handy with woodworking. Unfinished or old furniture may be cleverly redesigned. Wood spindles and wood trims are all available in lumber shops. Wood surfaces are covered with squares of overlapped papier-mâché in an almost random fashion. String is used to decorate drawer fronts and details around handles. Animals at top can be modeled in clay, then covered with papier-mâché. When dry, the paper shell is cut in half and the clay removed. Each half is finished. The result is two facing figures. The central top motif can be modeled with wet papier or instant mâché over a wood shape, then mounted in place.

Courtesy, Clark & Burchfield, Inc., Los Angeles

chapter 6

Papier-Mâché for Furniture and Furnishings

Mention "papier-mâché" furniture and most people furrow their brow and conjure a picture of flimsy, easily breakable, novelty items. Not so. Papier-mâché for furniture and furnishings opens up a complete realm of new textures and finishes for unfinished or outmoded furniture that require a new coat. For furnishings, the potential of papier-mâché is wide open to imagination and invention. Entire rooms can be coordinated with papier-mâché as a decorating technique.

Papier-mâché furniture is not really new. In 1772, Henry Clay of Birmingham, England, patented a method of preparing paper pulp for building coaches, doors, panels, and furniture. Later it came into use as a substitute for plaster used to mold ornamentation of the rooms in eighteenth-century European rococo-styled homes. Eventually, the industry, based on hand decoration and molding, died out as industrialization methods took over.

Today's use of papier-mâché for furniture is not based on the molded paper technique of the eighteenth century. Instead, it is the same technique used to cover boxes and other items shown in Chapter One. It's the application that is inventive and beautiful.

Given an old piece of furniture that is too chipped and scratched to refinish by conventional furniture finishing techniques of sanding, varnishing, etc., one can cover all the blemishes quickly, economically, and attractively with torn pieces of paper glued in a pattern. The pieces are then sealed, decorated, and painted. Or create your own cabinets, shelves, etc., from inexpensive wood and then finish with papier-mâché. Assorted, novel textures may be achieved by using various kinds of papers such as paper towels, packing paper, plastic bubble paper, etc.

Once you learn the potential of papier-mâché for furniture you won't want to throw away a thing. You can also expand the shape of any existing piece of furniture by adding to it with a simple armature, then developing a desired shape with a base of easy-to-shape aluminum foil, as shown beginning on page 163.

Little preparation of the base piece is required. At the most, one

BUFFET. Squares of paper slightly overlapped create the texture and finish in this large chest which has bookshelves above. Stylized flowers are simply added shapes of tagboard glued in low relief. Chest is a lively pink with green, deep pink, and orchid flowers. Objects on chest are also of papier-mâché.

Photographed at Sala de Artes, Mexico City

should sand or rasp cabinet doors and drawers so they will close after the layers of paper are put on them, and remove any rusty, protruding nails. Entire walls have been done in papier-mâché as a backdrop for a piece; and only lack of a wide-angle lens prevented photographing such a room in a California home.

Furnishings can be beautifully coordinated with papier-mâché because you are controlling color and design in your own inimitable, creative taste. Old lamps can be redesigned by shaping new paper around them or by building a disliked form into another shape. Entire new lamps can be made from a shape of cardboard as though it's an armature. It's amazing how a walk down an alley on a day when people throw things out can result in "finds" you can cover with papier-mâché and treasure for years.

In addition to the items illustrated to stimulate your application of papier-mâché, think in terms of the designs, textures, and patterns you can create on basement walls, on kitchen splashboards, on barrels, cubes, and large wire cores easily converted to furniture. With imagination, there's no limit to the kinds of things you can create and renew with papier-mâché.

Chest of drawers has been completely refinished with a layer of "Teri" paper toweling which has nylon threads through it. Its texture and strength combined with glue, gesso, paint, and glazes makes it extremely tough and durable. By Susan Meilach.

A sheet of paper toweling is dipped in glue and applied as one large square overlapping another.

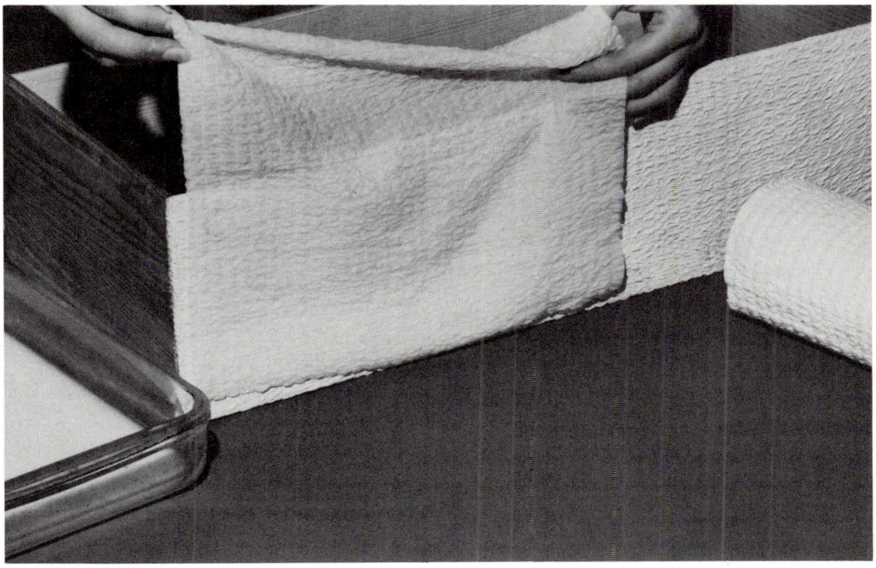

A piece of discarded furniture is given a new life and years of usability when covered with the papier-mâché technique. This chest as it appeared when found in an alley.

The oilcloth covering was removed; door edges rasped to allow for the space needed when layers of paper build up edges. All dust and sanding particles should be wiped off.

Bogus paper, much like construction paper, is bonded to the wood with wheat paste and white glue. The paper is dipped in water first to soften, then brushed with the glue mixture. Glue also may be brushed directly on surface, but paper must be reglued where edges overlap. After gluing, smooth out and distribute any built-up glue by going over papers with dampened brush. Allow paper to dry thoroughly.

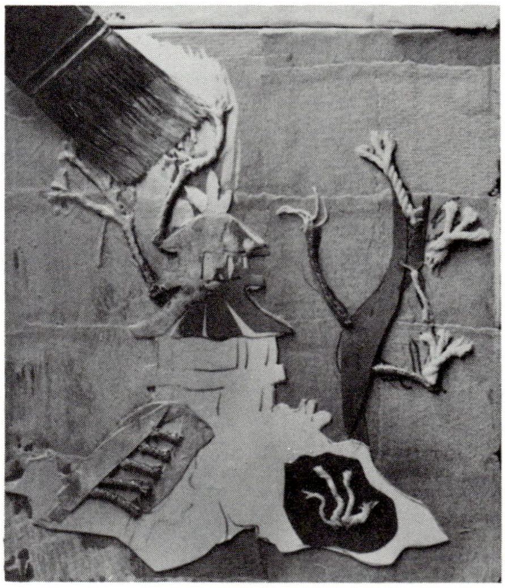

A design is built up of cardboard and string in the always popular Chinoiserie (in the Chinese manner) pagoda and tree composition. Three-ply seine twine is used because the plies can be separated and glued to splay out as branches. (See page 25, Chapter One.)

The entire chest is first sealed with one coat of gesso, being careful not to obliterate the texture of the torn paper edges. After the gesso dries the chest is painted with a coat of yellow gloss enamel. The details are hand painted. The entire chest may be antiqued, depending upon the final finish desired. Antiquing glaze is sprayed on, then quickly wiped off so only a light trace of it remains along papers' edges. Do not use lacquer over enamels as it will wrinkle the enamel. If a matte finish is desired, apply a flat enamel instead of a gloss and use a final coat of satin varnish. Always be sure that finishes used over paint coats are compatible.

The finished chest. Dona Meilach.

Twin-size headboard can be cut to shape on a jigsaw from any kind of wood, then covered with papier-mâché and a string design. Squares of paper are neatly overlapped. Vase and flowers are made with string, and areas filled in with paint.

Photographed at Los Castillo, Mexico City

Detail of decorating on the front of a cabinet. Only string is used to create the floral and bow outlines, then hand painting is added inside the leaves. The piece is antiqued and glazed.

Photographed at Los Castillo, Mexico City

HEADBOARDS designed by Mura Bright use large rectangles of paper overlapped and laid out in an angular pattern for great textural interest. Designs can be drawn from wallpaper to match a room; from gift wrap, from small details of favorite paintings, or from your own imagination. They may be drawn on paper first, then traced onto the headboard and worked with string and relief shapes of cardboard. Ready-made wood trims may be glued on too.

Courtesy, Clark & Burchfield, Inc., Los Angeles

CHEST AND HUTCH. Mura Bright. Controlled application of heavy papers add a texture and pattern unique to papier-mâché.

Courtesy, Clark & Burchfield, Inc., Los Angeles

BOOKSHELVES. Irene Nelson. Half-inch plywood and lathe-turned spindles are assembled for a bookshelf created inexpensively to fit a specific area. All plywood is covered with papier-mâché and finished with a deep mustard-color paint to coordinate with the color scheme of the room. One has to look closely to see that the shelves are finished with papier-mâché. But the surface is so rich-looking it has the appearance of a piece of fine, custom-made furniture.

Detail of shelf covered with papier-mâché.

Create a matching suite of furniture using the papier-mâché decorating technique with a design developed from glued string. Unfinished furniture has been painted and antiqued. Decorations may be hand painted or colored paper worked into the shapes. The entire chest is varnished. The chest, matching headboard, and dressing table are attractive, functional, and different.

Photographed at Sala de Artes, Mexico City

Outdoor furniture can be decorated with papier-mâché also. Take an old wrought-iron table, or any other weather-beaten furniture and redo it with papier-mâché for a colorful, durable treatment. Use polyurethane for the final coats over the papier-mâché to make the surfaces weather resistant. On this table, layers of torn newspaper were applied first to cover the tabletop. These were sealed and painted. Shapes of colored variegated tissues were added to create the design. These were sealed with a coat of transparent white glue so the colors would not be obliterated. Then six coats of polyurethane were applied. Heavy twisted cord at the edge is decorative and also prevents glasses and dishes from sliding off. The base is painted black.

Photographed at Sala de Artes, Mexico City

Patio table is covered with papier-mâché. Large leaves are made of cardboard. The center is built up with modeling paste or plaster and twine with colorful stones embedded. Cord is placed at the edge. The entire piece is colorfully painted in pinks, greens, and black, then the surface preserved with three coats of polyurethane, the same material used to preserve the hulls of boats and make them impervious to weather and water.

Photographed at Sala de Artes, Mexico City

ARCHED DOORS. Phyllis Peterson. Half-inch plywood cut to fit an odd-shaped doorway, and papier-mâchéd, is functional and ornamental. Two layers of tiny squares of papier-mâché simulate the appearance of an antique crazed surface. Designs are built up with pottery clay (do not use plasteline clay as it will not dry beneath paper), and the clay covered with papier-mâché. Clay will dry and remain under the paper. Seal, paint, and varnish. As glued papers dry, support the plywood on a flat surface and weight corners with rocks or bricks, if necessary, to prevent slab of wood from warping. Designs on doors are different on front and back.

Detail of crest on door with plaster cupid purchased from a clay house.

Detail of squiggles at top of door built up with pottery clay, covered with paper, rope added, then the entire door and details painted. By Phyllis Peterson.

WRITING DESK. Lucy Anderson. Newspaper, string, and easy-to-do hand painting give an old writing desk a completely new life. Subtly finished in wood tones with a hint of color, the piece livens a small corner.

CORNICE. Phyllis Peterson. Three pieces of plywood glued together and decorated in the same way as the doors (page 158) are easily created. It is hung with picture hangers and repeats colors in the draperies.

TABLE. Irene Nelson. With only squares of paper, glue, paint, and decorating fringe, an old table was saved. Two-inch squares of torn construction paper were glued in a radiating pattern beginning from the center. The edge is drapery-trim fringe which was dipped in blue and attached. The table was sealed and painted. Light gold paint, antiquing glaze, and a final satin varnish coat magically simulates the look of old leather.

Put a kangaroo in your child's bedroom made over an old piece of furniture. The success of the piece depends upon the capacity of Alcoa aluminum foil to be molded, then hammered tightly before covering with paper toweling as the papier-mâché medium. The overall design is finished with a layer of paper tablecloth, already decorated, dipped in glue and worked over the paper towels.

Designed by Conny of Alcoa
Photos, courtesy, Aluminum Company of America

1. Nail a dowel rod and two supporting strips of wood to the back of the chest. Tape the wood strips to the dowel rod.

2. Begin to shape the body of the kangaroo with the aluminum foil by wrapping and crumbling. It is extremely moldable. Even the high tail tightly wound and shaped is strong enough to be self-supporting. Build up form, continuing to cover with additional sheets of foil to hold parts such as arms, neck, tail, etc., in place.

3. Add foil to round out the hips, mold ears, etc. Then hammer the foil with a large mallet or side of hammer until it holds a solid form.

4. Rear view of molded kangaroo form after aluminum foil has been hammered to give the form solidity.

5. Place wrinkle-free, wheat-paste-soaked sheets of paper towels on figure, overlapping and making as smooth as possible. This gives the figure a smoother base than the foil and a white underlining. As the final decoration will be predesigned paper and not paint, no sealer is required.

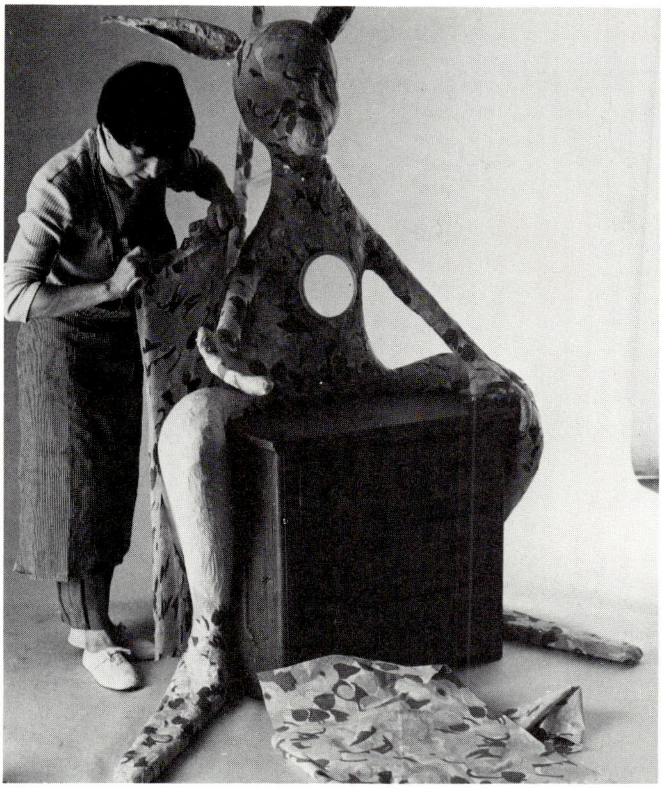

6. Glue and place pieces of decorative material on the pasted paper towels cutting and working them around the kangaroo form. The covering surface material may be paper tablecloths or napkins readily available in a marvelous range of designs and colors. They are soft and moldable when wet.

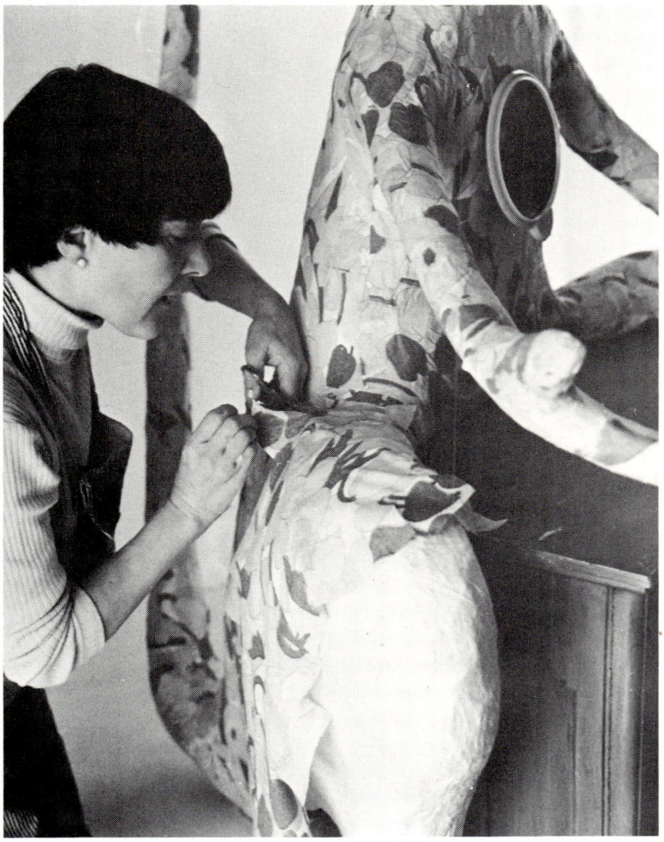

7. Make slashes where needed for a neat fit. For solid colors over the ear and the tip of the nose, use several layers of colored art tissue paper. Cover entire piece with thin layer of white glue diluted with water in about a half and half ratio. Add pieces of felt for eyebrows and eyes. Paint on nostrils. Hang a mirror on the kangaroo's chest. (See finished piece.) Other figures on chest are made over large cans and built up with foil. The top of the chest is covered with the same paper. The chest may be painted a complementary color and the entire piece finished with a clear spray glaze, lacquer, or satin varnish.

Look what grew into a giraffe under the imaginative hands of Conny of Alcoa. A stepladder became the base for the tall, long-necked creature that is strong enough for a child to play upon. A dowel rod extended from the base is ample support for the molded and hammered aluminum foii neck created in the same way as the kangaroo and covered with paper tablecloths. A stool with a dowel placed through a hole drilled in the seat is the base for the smaller figure which also provides a seat for the children to "ride" upon. Make his neck turn slightly, if you like, for an even more whimsical look. For the mane, glue several strips of paper together, fringe, and stick to back of neck.

Courtesy, Aluminum Company of America

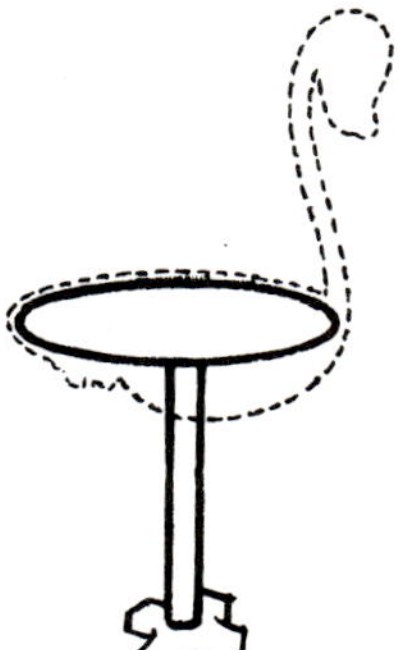

FIREPLACE SCREEN. Dona Ziegler. To make a fireplace opening more attractive when not in use, place a brightly decorated papier-mâché screen in front of it made over a piece of plywood. Dona Ziegler gessoes the wood to seal it, then covers it with one large sheet of colored tissue paper for background color. Daisies, leaves, stems, and butterfly are cut out, sealed, and then pasted in bas-relief technique. Decorations are hand painted, the screen is antiqued, then sprayed with several coats of glaze. Hardware is attached to the back.

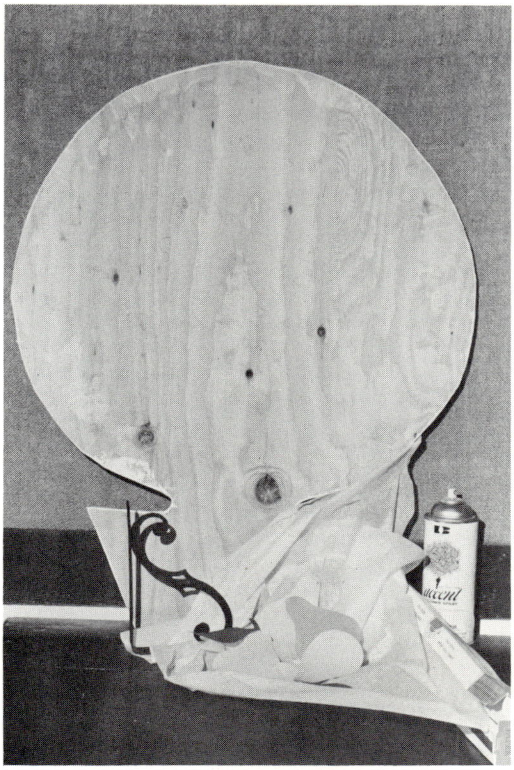

Materials needed to make a fireplace screen are a piece of wood cut to shape and slightly larger than the area to be covered; tissue paper, shirt cardboard for cutouts, a corner bracket, necessary paints, and glaze finishes.

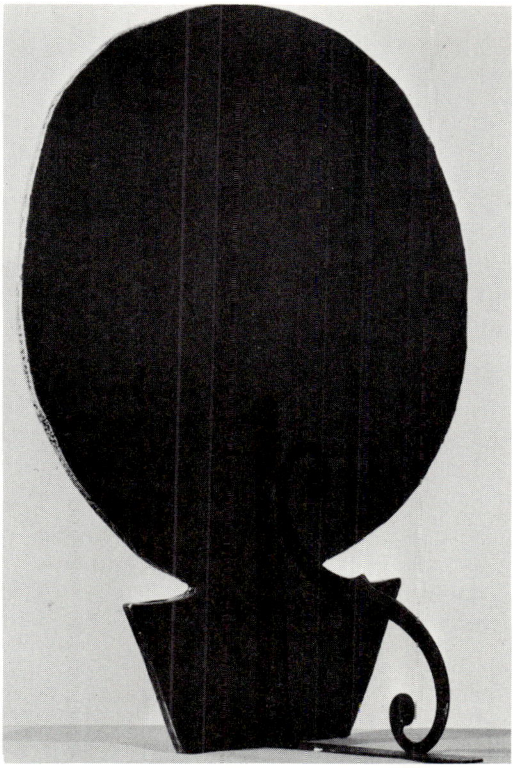

Back of screen with corner bracket in place to make it stand up. Back should be papered and finished with a complementary color.

Antiquing is applied with a damp sponge and built up stronger around the cutout patterns. A screen may be any design—the spread feather of an ostrich, an open fan, an entire flower, a repeat of a pattern or a detail from a painting elsewhere in the room. As long as you're cutting the design from wood, you can make it any shape you like.

WIG STAND LAMP. Irene Nelson. Papier-mâché over a Styrofoam head is wired and made into a lamp. To heighten and weight the lamp, tape it to a base of wood or plaster, marble or metal. The entire head and base are covered with papier-mâché, then sealed with two to six coats of gesso if a very smooth ceramic look is desired. Or gesso may be placed directly on the plastic foam to seal, then the design added with string, paper, etc. Shapes for hair, eyebrows, moustache, and nose may be made with instant mâché, or wadded-up aluminum foil or moist paper pulp that is moldable. To achieve a higher gloss on the face, paint full-strength white glue on the area where the highest shine is desired. Hand paint details and glaze with preferred product.

LAMPS

Further evidence of the versatility of papier-mâché is illustrated by the lamps on the following pages; all made with methods already shown for the use of papier-mâché. Some are made over existing lamps that are outmoded and which the owner has tired of. Others are made over objects associated with another use, then captured by artistic imagination and the urge to be creative. Still others are designed from heavy paper so they will either stand by themselves or be supported by a dowel or a brass tube screwed to a base. Lamps must allow for necessary wiring and shade holders.

Component lamp parts may be purchased in a hardware store so that creating your own lamp is really simple. Lightweight bases, such as Styrofoam wig stands, should be weighted by embedding a rock in the base or attaching a piece of stone, wood, or metal to the bottom.

Lampshades from the dime store may be trimmed to repeat the colors and designs of the base. If they are to be covered with paper, use a transparent art tissue so the light will come through. They may also be spray painted.

Essentially, all the techniques already learned for papier-mâché in Chapters One and Two are used for making lamps.

Component parts for a lamp are a Styrofoam wig stand, which requires a hole through the center for the brass tube to hold the wire, the brass tube, socket, harp, wire, and plug.

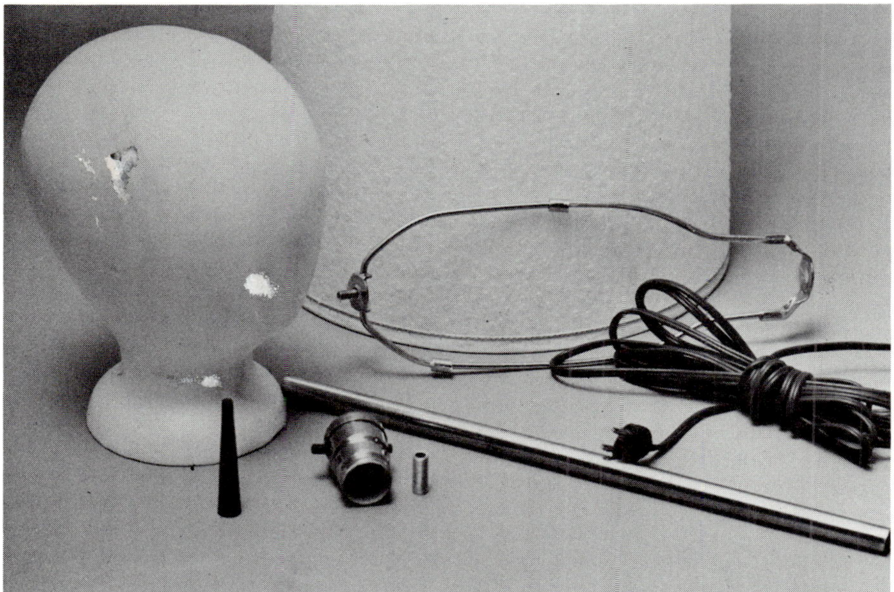

GIRL WITH THE HORN OF PLENTY. Bob Lee. You can make a lamp as colorful, whimsical, and happy as this one. Use heavy kraft paper to fashion a large and a small cornucopia. Use the large one for the body, tape the small one to the large to hold the bundle of plenty. Double a piece of kraft and make a cylinder for the head. Cut two cardboard circles and place one at each end of the cylinder. One becomes the face and the other the back of the head. Slit cylinder from rear and work to fit around lamp pole. Tape all parts together. (For smaller lamps, the head might be made from an empty oatmeal box.) Add paper toweling for the mâché texture and to cover taped joints. Hand paint as desired. Mr. Lee uses designer's gouache for a matte finish as opposed to glaze finishes. This lamp might also be made over a wired rod or over an old lamp.

Rear view of Bob Lee's Horn of Plenty lamp. For designs and facial expressions, the artist often consults children's book illustrations.

The understructure is fashioned from heavy kraft paper; the parts are taped together, then covered with papier-mâché.

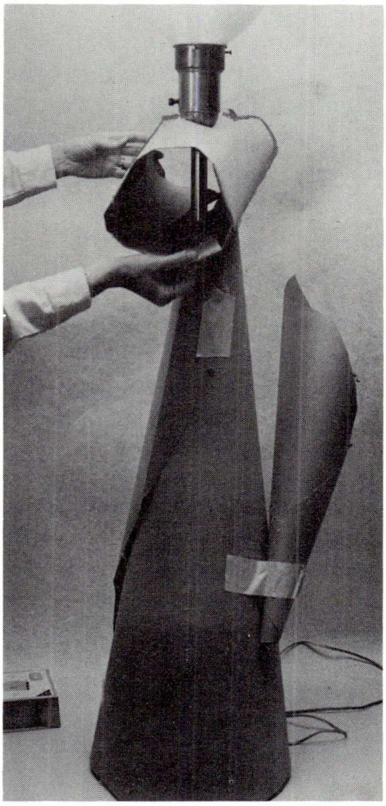

FLOWER GIRL. Bob Lee. The same procedures for creating the girl with the Horn of Plenty are used to create her companion carrying a basket of flowers. Arms are shaped of cardboard taped to the body and to the flowerpot.

Side view of lamp.

The angelic lamp by Bob Lee also relies on the cone shape, but the head is more oval. Wings and arms of cardboard are attached. The flounce, also of cardboard, is added around the base of the lamp. To weight a lamp made from component parts, Mr. Lee may use a plaster cone with a hole through the middle for wiring. A paper cone shape is glued on the plaster cone.

A gnome lamp by Bob Lee, complete with checkered gloves, is still a basic cone shape with collar, ears, and hat with gifts added. Actually, all the lamps are easy to make. Depending upon one's taste and decorating scheme, the same basic shape could be varied to create lamps in any style from rococo to contemporary and even simulate a wide variety of natural finishes . . . and all with paper.

Detail of lamp base.

Another lamp style created with papier-mâché is developed to resemble china. An armature is made over a lamp pole in the same methods shown in Chapter Two. Figure may be molded from aluminum foil, then covered with glue-dipped paper and materials to make a "skirt that seems to billow in the breeze." Laces dipped in glue are used for the underslip. The piece is highly glazed yet retains a rough texture. Additional texture may be added by applying a thin coat of plaster in a rippling effect over the skirt to contrast with the smooth face which has a glaze coat of white glue.

Detail of shade shows that it has been covered with squares of transparent tissue papier-mâché for additional texture. The lace around edge repeats the pattern in the slip.

Lamp photographed in Mexico

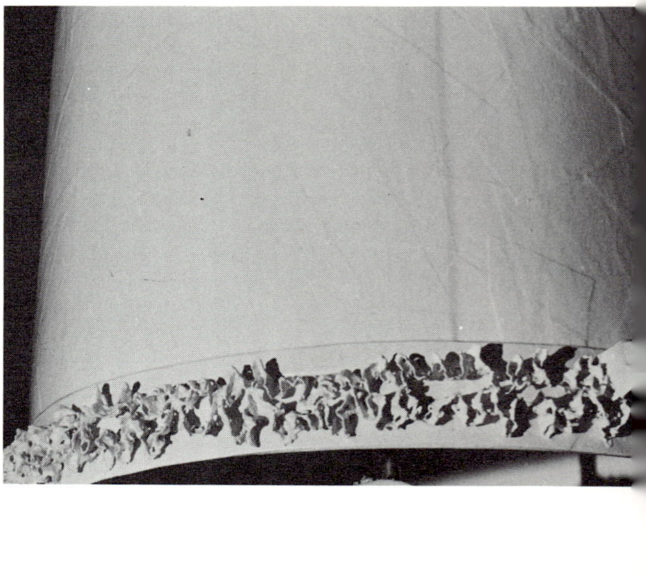

ART NOUVEAU LAMPSHADES. Bob Lee. These are made over ready-made thin sheet-metal blanks available in lamp shops. Thin cardboard, cut, scored, and bent can also be developed into similar shapes, papier-mâchéd and decorated.

Photo, Bob Lee

An old lamp may be reshaped using the papier-mâché methods. The scratched, outmoded metal base was filled in with glue-dipped paper toweling and mashed aluminum foil to eliminate the feet and the brass balls.

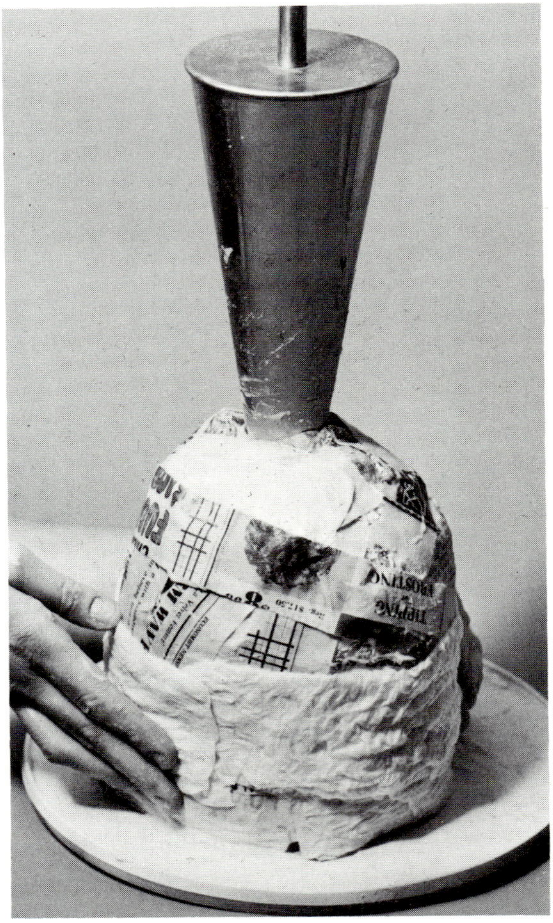

The top conical shape was changed to a straight cylinder with a roll of stiff paper and layers of newspaper strips. The bottom portion was covered with newspaper strips also, then the lamp dried for several days in the sun. It could be force-dried on a radiator or in front of a hot-air vent for several days also.

Snail-like forms were made of two layers of construction paper with a strip of armature wire through the middle to hold the bend firm. Each "curl" was taped to the neck of lamp. String, glued around the base, repeats the design of the curls.

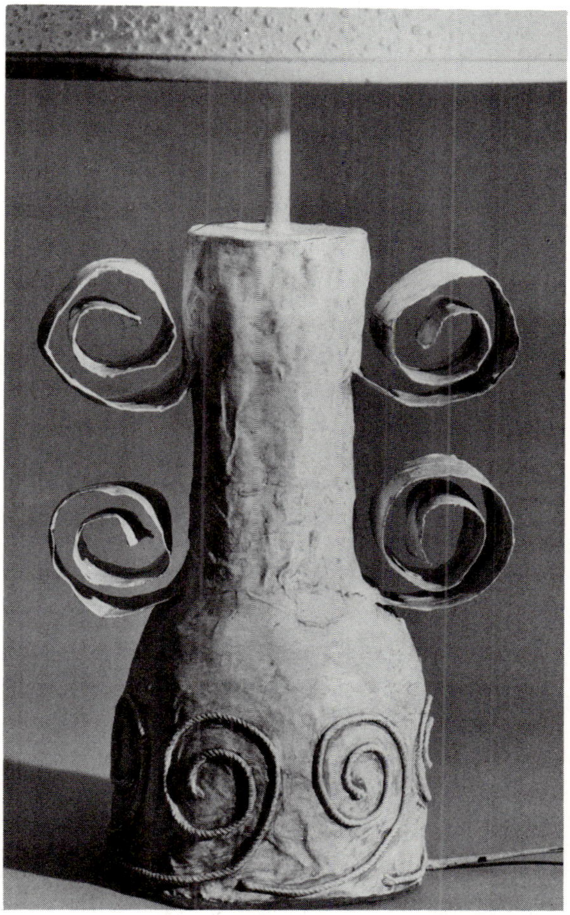

The base was gessoed, then sprayed with yellow matte enamel, then antiqued. The old lampshade also was renewed and matched with spray and antique treatment. A final glaze gave the lamp a porcelain appearance. By Lynn Zweigoron.

Students of James Seidelman mold papier-mâché over balloons and light bulbs to create heads for puppets.

Courtesy, James Seidelman & Grace Mintonye

chapter 7

Papier-Mâché by and for Young People

Among the versatile aspects of papier-mâché is its adaptability to projects at every age, experience, and ability level. From early primary grades through sophisticated approaches to creativity at an art school, papier-mâché can be used to express ideas, form, shape, color, and design. Whether students are five or twenty, the basic techniques already presented in Chapters One, Two, and Three are the same. Children readily grasp the idea of forming an armature from assorted materials such as stuffed paper bags, taped cardboard tubes, paper cups, paper plates, cigar boxes, Styrofoam, bottles, cardboard, rolled lengths of paper, wire, and all combinations of these that they may conjure for a finished shape.

They may use the covering technique and renew an existing shape in its entirety giving it a different context. Working with molds also is recommended for upper-grade students who can sustain interest and follow through the three procedures required: creating the original, making the mold, and lining the mold with paper to make the casting.

For classroom groups, the easiest, least expensive pastes are flour and water or wheat paste and water. They are easy to clean up.

Children may be encouraged to work with papier-mâché as a form of self-expression, as a decorative art, and as a practical art for puppet shows, carnivals, geography maps, dioramas, theatrical productions, and as an adjunct to relief forms in collage and assemblage constructions.

The examples shown are created primarily by students in grammar, junior high, and high school. Jewelry and vanity accessories are included as possible projects that would appeal to young people.

Animal heads in a variety of shapes and final trim all began from folded and stuffed paper armatures taped and built up with more paper, paste, and tape. The evolution of the forms may be seen at right.

From the same kind of form, the student can mold the head to represent an animal or human shape: He can add ears, trim, and expression that are individually his own creation.

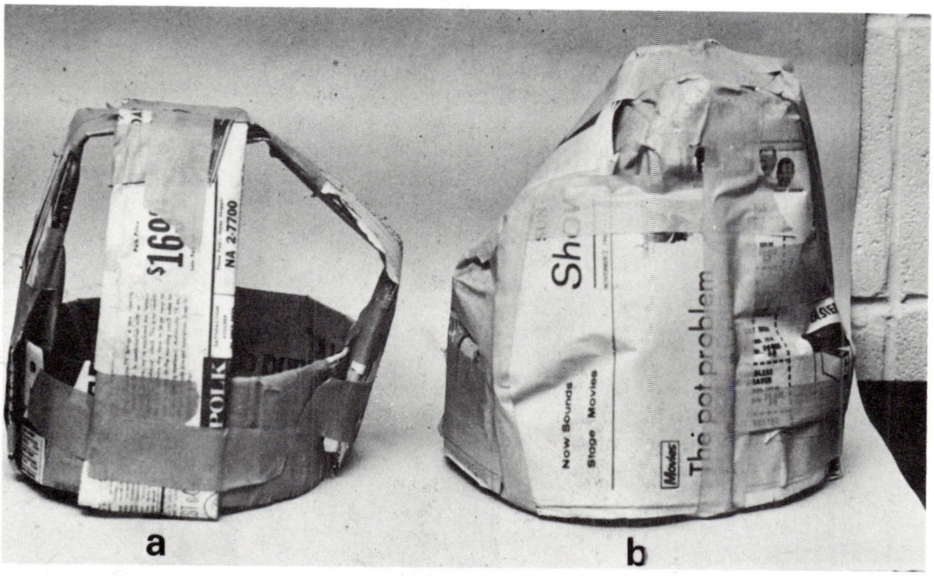

The armature begins by (A) folding newspaper and taping it together with masking tape. (B) The form is further developed by adding more folded paper and taping it together for rigidity.

(C) An animal head begins to emerge complete with taped-on ears. (D) Another shape has been created. Finishing depends on the child's initiative, teacher direction, and availability of materials. In the examples, some of the heads have been covered with a glued coat of papier-mâché squares before painting, others are given several coats of gesso and then painted. Still others rely on a layer of art tissue for a base color, then painting proceeds.

Student examples from Carol Briscoe's classes
Fry School, South Stickney, Illinois

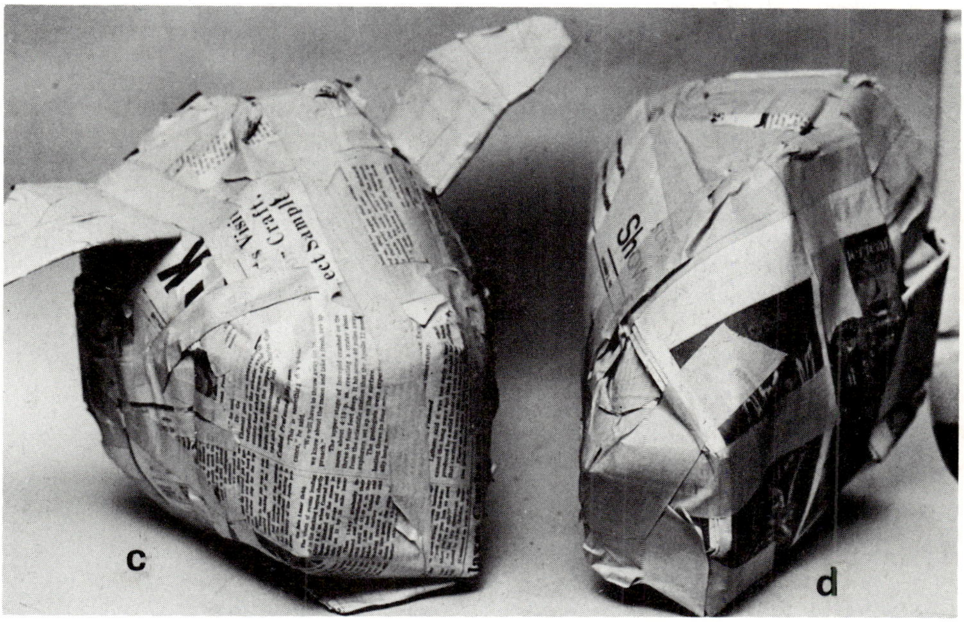

PENGUIN

Seventh and eighth grade students of Carol Briscoe have expressed a variety of observations in the sculptural use of papier-mâché over armatures of folded and taped newspaper.

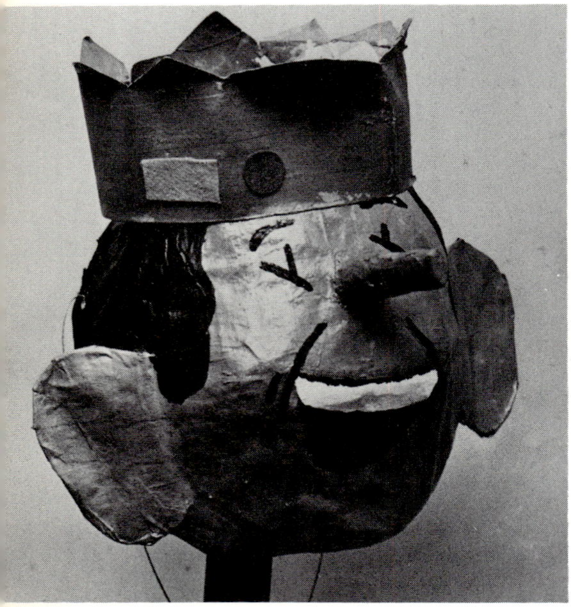

COMEDIAN

SPORTSMAN

SAILFISH

TURTLE

Puppets with papier-mâché heads have easy-to-make costumes which combine many learning experiences.

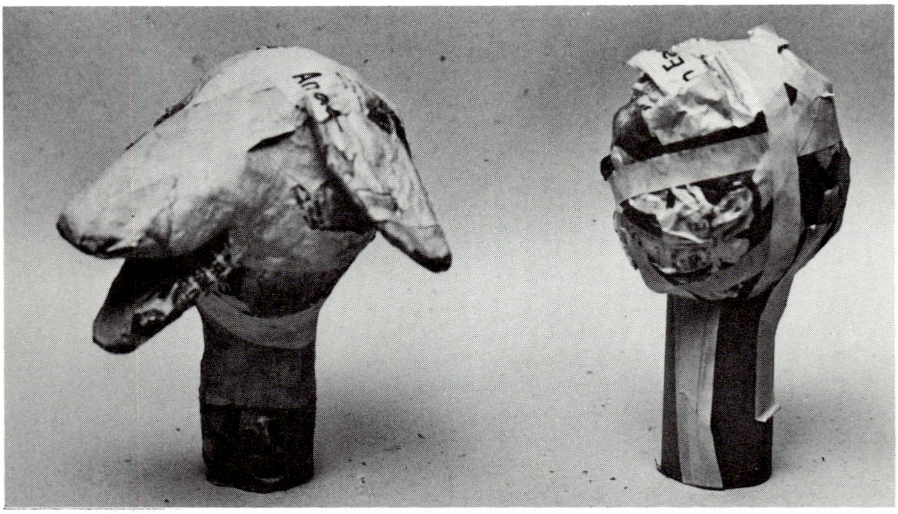

Puppets' heads may also be formed from wadded paper over a cardboard tube which is used for the fingers to reach up and manipulate the puppet's action. The head may be only wadded paper or it could be formed over a balloon, light bulb, or Styrofoam ball. Teachers, aware of all the possibilities, are free to improvise, depending on availability of materials.

Students of Carol Briscoe

BIG BROWN APE WITH BANANA. Sharon Karp. Form is of shaped chicken wire covered with paste-soaked strips of papier-mâché, then gessoed, painted brown, and glazed with varnish.

College level work

FISH OUT OF WATER is made over a rolled paper base and given a textured finish by mixing sand with the gesso before applying, then painting with colors. Fins are added cardboard.

College level work

Papier-mâché over bottles. All examples by students of Karlo Harootunian, sixth to eighth grades, Fairview South School, Skokie, Illinois.

PAPIER-MÂCHÉ OVER BOTTLES

Bottles of all sizes, shapes, and materials offer one of the most readily available sources for work by both students and adults. The younger child may begin by covering a bottle and simply painting a face on it. He learns what papier-mâché can accomplish in transforming one object to another. He may progress to taping shapes to the bottle with newspaper or cardboard, or wads of wet newspaper used as instant mâché. Or he may apply ready-made instant mâché for details. Shown above are several imaginative uses for bottles that once held food and laundry products, library paste, etc.

Be sure the glue medium used will hold the paper to the bottle; some plastic and waxed bottles repel water-base glue products although undiluted white emulsion glue almost always holds. If glue does not hold, the bottle can be wrapped with masking tape, then covered with paper.

A laundry bleach jar has been creatively visualized and decorated to become a gnome. For the rough texture, instant papier-mâché was used over the bottle and over wire added for the arms. Flat feet of cardboard add an ingenious, humorous touch.

This paste jar is all dressed up complete with bow tie and black hat.

Children need little encouragement to exercise their imaginations when given free rein to develop the use of papier-mâché.

Bottles may be combined with shaped cardboard or paper to extend a form. The center of this huge fish is a large wine bottle. The front is an oatmeal box that has been cut away for the mouth, the tail is simply rolled and tapered corrugated cardboard taped over the neck of the bottle.

In the same fashion as above, a quart-size soda bottle became the body for the alligator.

Students of Karlo Harootunian

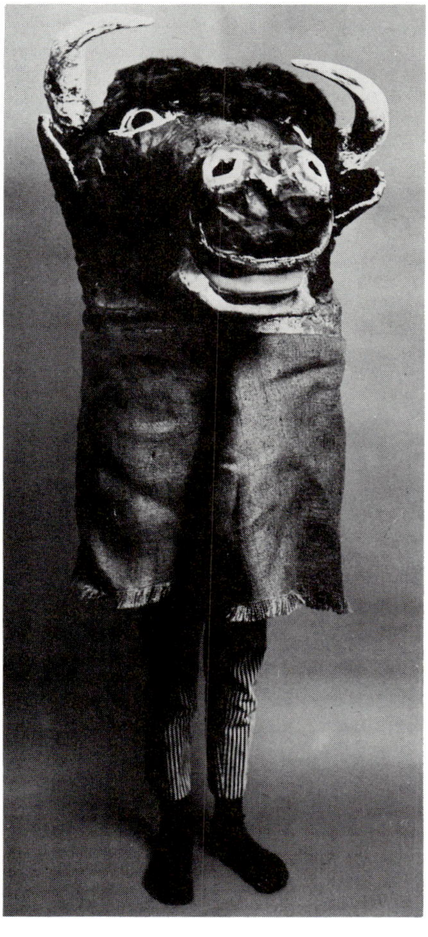

A hobby horse by Kay Whitcomb Keith could be easily simulated by anyone anxious to keep a child amused. The head is formed over paper, then covered with papier-mâché strips. The mane is a mop that has had a haircut.

Photo, Glasheen Graphics

MASK AND COSTUME. Bonnie Henricks. A chicken-wire shape was made to fit over her son's head, then combined with a costume to match.

Courtesy, Illinois Bronze Paint Company

DONUT by William Striz is made of newspaper formed into coils and held with glued paper. A thin coat of plaster was applied over the entire piece with heavier plaster buildup for the frosting. Color is tempera with polymer for a glaze. The CUPCAKE by Ellen Balfanz is made from a bushel basket stuffed with newspaper. Chicken wire over the top is covered with papier-mâché and plaster. Fluted paper forms the cupcake wrapper.

TELEPHONE. Karen Martarno. Made from cardboard covers, tubes, and cut shapes covered with newspaper dipped in wheat paste, dried, and painted black.

PENCIL. Steve Vandivier. Shaped cardboard with point made from a cone of paper; plastic foam is used for the eraser.

ICE CREAM CONE. Peter Vina. Made over a newspaper cone and newspaper stuffed paper bags for the ice cream. Yarn is glued to cone to simulate a real cone.

All examples from students of Lorraine Ohlson, Proviso East High School, Maywood, Illinois

BRACELETS, JEWELRY, AND HAND MIRRORS

Jewelry pieces such as bracelets, earrings, and rings are easy and fun to make. Results can be as varied as one likes from rough-textured mâché pulp to smooth-as-china finishes. Hand mirrors are also an easy-to-create item popular with young girls.

For jewelry, one needs jewelry findings: that is, pin backings, earring screws, cuff link backs, and rings. For pendants, you will need chains, all readily available from craft suppliers. The technique shown may be adapted to any individualized jewelry designs.

Hand mirrors require blanks of wood or heavy cardboard cut to desired shapes, then papier-mâchéd and decorated by any of the techniques shown in Chapter One.

A soda can or bottle is the perfect size for making bracelets for adults. For children use a baby-food bottle. Grease or talc the bottle so the papier-mâché will not stick to it. Then (A) wrap a strip of newspaper around the bottle in the width of the bracelet you want to make. (B) Add squares of construction paper over this strip for extra strength, then about six additional layers of papier-mâché. (C) Remove from bottle. If you want the bracelet curved, shape it while wet. You can also make it appear curved by placing a folded strip of paper around the center of the outside, then covering that with more papier-mâché. Dry.

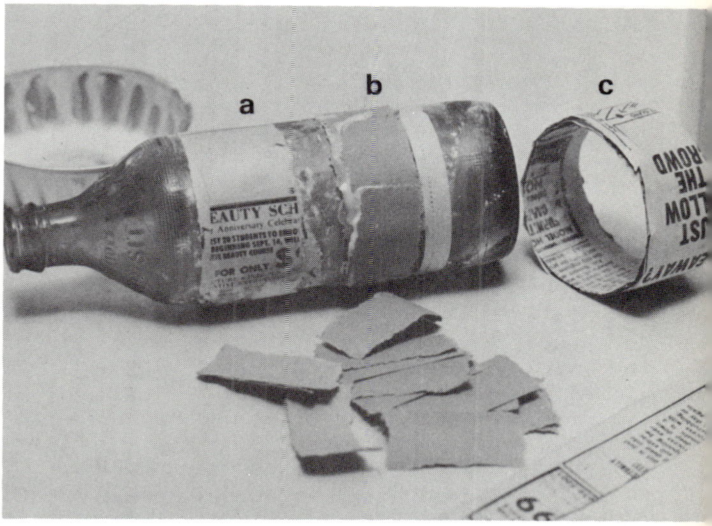

For a finished edge, trim with a sharp knife or with scissors and fold another piece of newspaper around the bracelet. Or sand the edge by rubbing it along a piece of sandpaper or a sanding block.

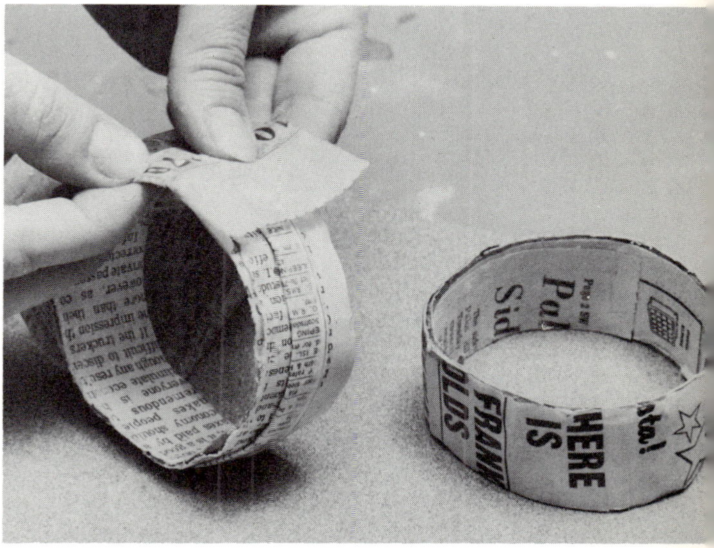

Seal the bracelet with gesso. Gesso will fill in the rough paper edges. Use several coats for a ceramic-like finish; allowing the gesso to dry between coats. Decorate with string, beads, stones, paint, or any novelty decorating materials such as this silver that comes from a tube.

Bracelets may be wide or narrow, rounded or flat. They may be painted with clear bright colors and then glazed; or they may be antiqued. Make bracelets to match individual outfits for a totally coordinated fashion appearance.

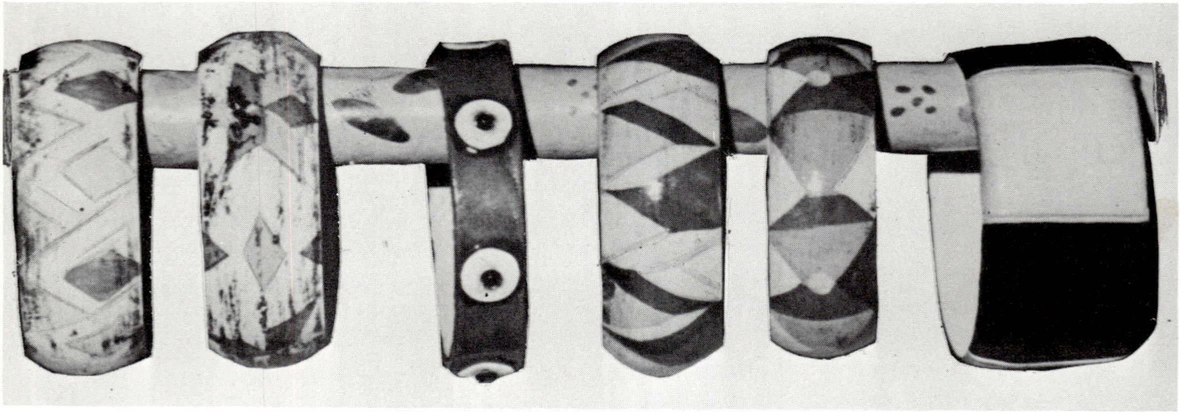

Pins and rings are formed in the same techniques used to make flower decorations for tops of boxes shown in Chapter One. Make them large or small, one or two layers, in any design you like. For flower shapes, refer to flower catalogs; for whimsical animal pictures, trace shapes from children's story books and coloring books. Illustrated story books also are good sources for colors to be used. For half-round shapes use half of a Styrofoam or table tennis ball.

Sometimes instant mâché and cardboard shapes do not adhere sufficiently to metal findings. Use extra-strength glue such as Duco-cement for holding objects to metal. When possible place a few narrow strips of paper around the finding and over the object for added strength. This should be done while making the jewelry, not after all parts are painted.

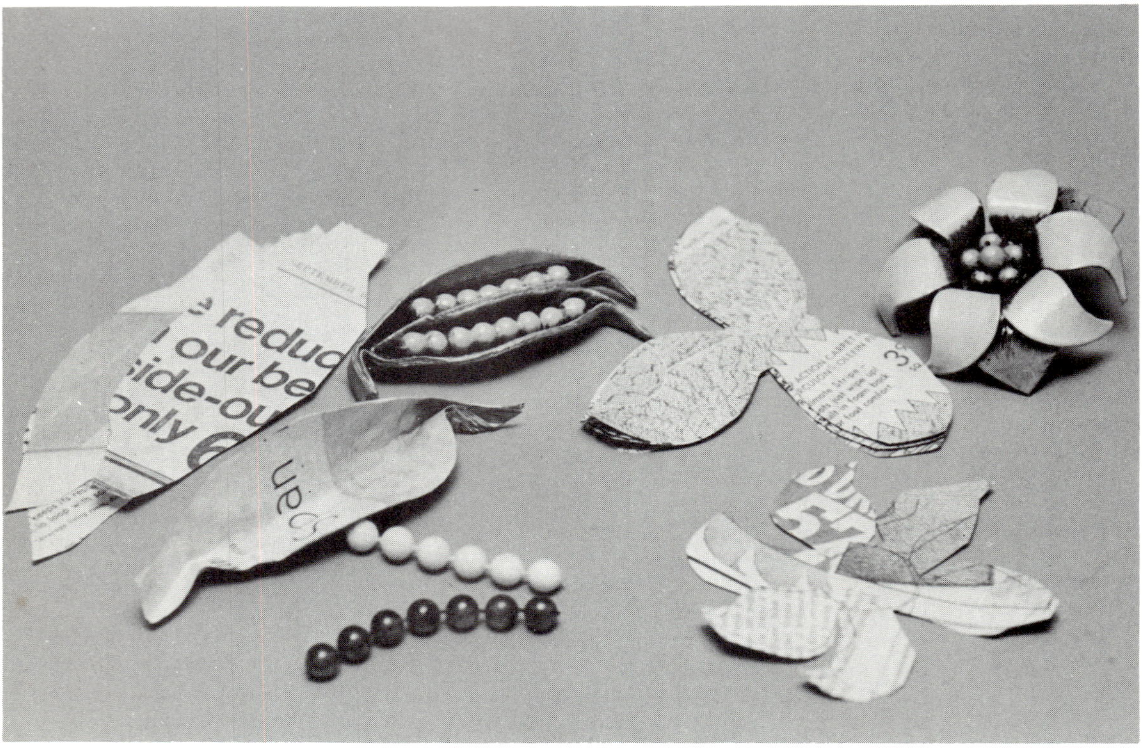

To create pins, rings, and earrings, follow the same techniques shown on page 26, Chapter One, for creating relief forms for decorating. Cut six layers of newsprint to desired shapes. Glue together, shape. Combine with larger and smaller layers. Continue in the same procedures for all papier-mâché: seal, decorate, paint, and glaze. Only, of course, tape or glue the necessary jewelry finding to the back of the object.

In the peapod pin, left, two sets of the peapod are made and glued together and shaped. After drying, sealing, and painting, beads are added to represent the peas.

For the pin, right, petals are cut from newsprint as shown. The bottom set of petals is like a clover: the upper set is made with six petals. They are bent while the glue is still wet and the finding glued to the back. After sealing, and finishing, the center beads are added. The entire pin is glazed and ready for wear.

Pins, rings, earrings are all made following these procedures.

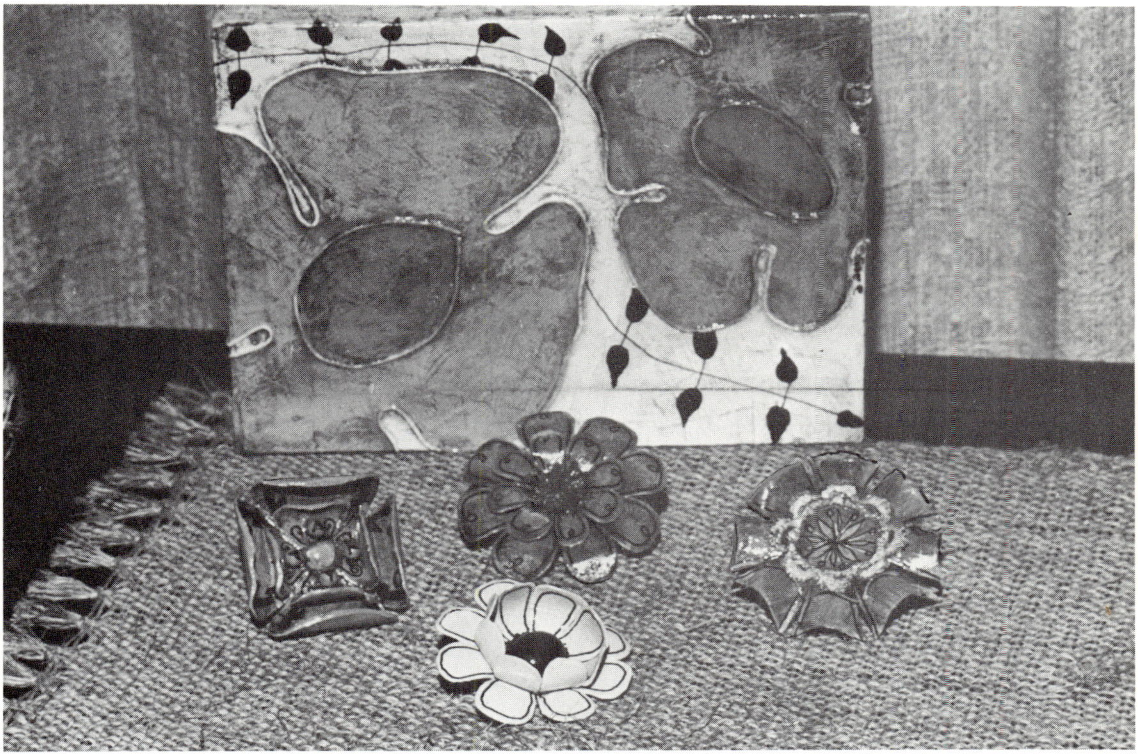

Pin shapes may be as varied as the flowers in your garden. In fact, real flowers are a good source for design and color too. Also observe photos in seed catalogs for flower shapes and colorations. Pins by Frances Gove.

Rings, too, are made from pasted shapes of paper worked to represent flowers. For more delicate tints, try covering some of these with art tissue paper.

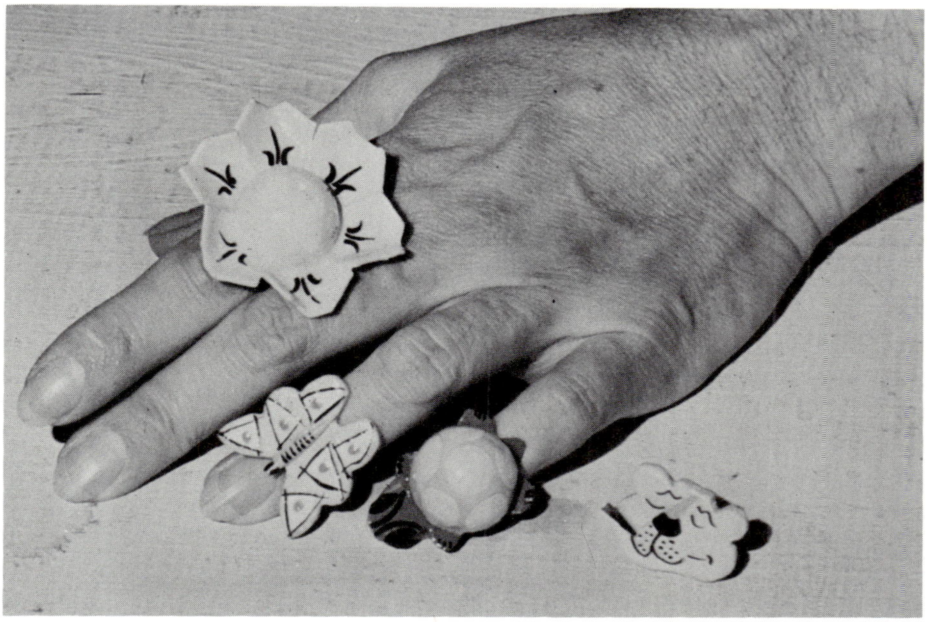

More rings made in shapes of bugs as well as flowers. For half balls, use plastic foam or instant mâché.

Earrings may be made large or small, rough and smooth. The hoops are made exactly as the bracelets, in size desired. For a rough finish cover with paper toweling or add instant mâché. The ball earrings may be rolled instant mâché or foil covered with papier-mâché.

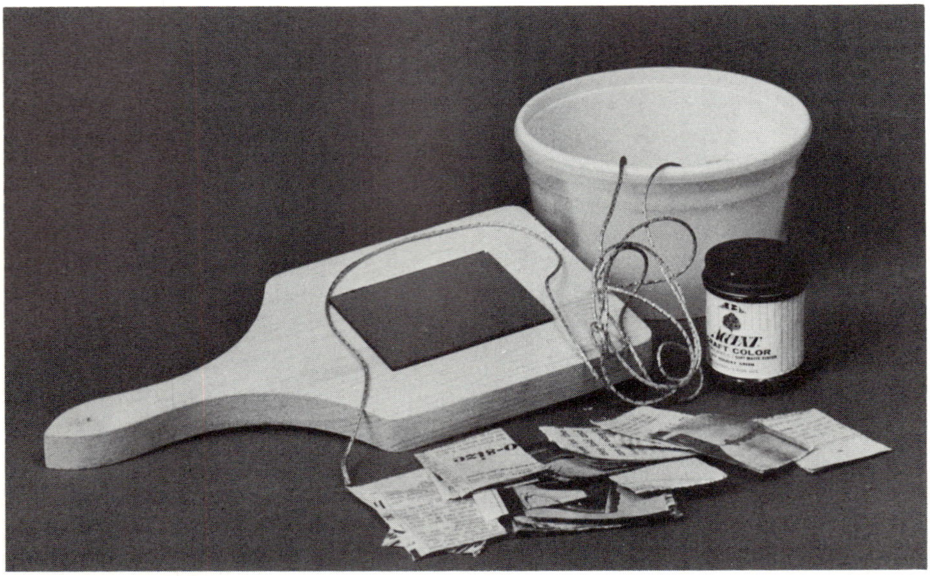

HAND MIRRORS may be created to match a room decor or other vanity pieces such as jewelry boxes, tissue dispensers, curler holders, or bottle covers. They may be made over precut and sanded pieces of lightweight pine using the same methods for covering, sealing, and decorating shown in Chapter One. Shapes may be cut from two or three layers of heavy cardboard glued together for rigidity, then covered with papier-mâché. They may be made over plastic dime-store mirrors, simply recovered and designed to your own tastes. When using ready-made mirrors, cover the mirror portion with masking tape while decorating to prevent paste and paint from spattering the glass.

Hand-mirror backs are attractively decorated.

Hand-mirror shapes can depart from conventional forms when you cut them yourself from wood or cardboard.

Index

H

I

J

K

L

M